DECIDING
TO LEAD

*The English Teacher
as Reformer*

DENNY WOLFE & JOE ANTINARELLA

Boynton/Cook Publishers

HEINEMANN

Portsmouth, NH

PE68
.U5
W65
1997

Boynton/Cook Publishers, Inc.
A subsidiary of Reed Elsevier Inc.
361 Hanover Street
Portsmouth, NH 03801-3912
Offices and agents throughout the world

The authors and publisher thank those who granted permission to use previously published material:
Parts of Chapter 2 originally appeared as "Three Approaches to Coping with School Violence" by Denny Wolfe. In *English Journal* (vol. 84, no. 5, September 1995). Copyright © 1995 by the National Council of Teachers of English. Reprinted with permission.
Poem 39 by Charles Reznikoff. Copyright © 1977 by Marie Syrkin Reznikoff. Reprinted from *Poems 1918–1975: The Complete Poems of Charles Reznikoff* with the permission of Black Sparrow Press.
Excerpts from "An Interview with James Gray" by Denny Wolfe. In *SLATE Newsletter* (vol. 18, no. 1, April 1993). Copyright © 1993 by the National Council of Teachers of English. Reprinted with permission.
Excerpts from a speech by James Britton, Old Dominion University, Norfolk, VA, August 15, 1978 (videotaped with Mr. Britton's permission). Printed by permission of Old Dominion University.

Library of Congress Cataloging-in-Publication Data
Wolfe, Denny T.
    Deciding to lead: the English teacher as reformer / Denny Wolfe and Joseph Antinarella.
        p. cm.
    ISBN 0-86709-402-6
    1. English philology—Study and teaching (Secondary)—United States.   2. Teacher participation in administration—United States.
    3. Education (Secondary)—United States—Administration.
    4. Language arts (Secondary)—United States   5. Educational change—United States.   6. English teachers—United States.
    I. Antinarella, Joseph C., 1953– .   II. Title.
    PE68.U5W65   1997   97-3436
    428'.0071'273—dc21   CIP

Editor: Peter Stillman
Cover design: Catherine Hawkes
Manufacturing: Louise Richardson

Printed in the United States of America on acid-free paper

00 99 98 97 DA 1 2 3 4 5 6

This book is dedicated
to
The National Writing Project,
an exemplary model of school reform
whose teacher-consultants
make a difference in America every day

Contents

Acknowledgments

The following, indispensable:

Fran Weinberg, George Steele, Betty Schindler, Jim Heinen, Catherine Pohlman, Tiziana Lohnes, Carroll Starling, Bob Lucking, Bob Reising, Bill Strong, Collett Dilworth, Joe Milner, Bob Shuman, Julian and Jane Heath, Bob MacDonald, Donna Evans, Bill Cunningham, Hilve Firek, Ben Brunwin, Amber Winkler, Bob Tierney, Don Gallehr, Nelson Lopez, Lee Manning, Ashley Todd, Cary Wolfe, Celia Wolfe, JoAnne Antinarella—all of whom helped and challenged in caring and unique ways, sometimes unaware.

All the teachers we know personally who permitted us into their worlds and whose work appears explicitly and implicitly throughout this book, but particularly—Ken Salbu, Ed Jacob, Bill Etzel, Beth Bond, Valerie Klauss, Charles Jarvis, Terri Darnell, Karen Reidelbach.

Peter Stillman, who pressed and above all counseled.

The wind in the willow.

Language gives us a way of belonging to each other.

Terry Eagleton, Oxford University
Keynote Address to the International
Conference, Global Conversations on
Language and Literacy
Heidelberg, Germany
August 12, 1996

No one here tonight would have traveled so far without teachers.
They are our real American heroes.

Evan Bayh
Governor of Indiana
Democratic National Convention
Chicago
August 27, 1996

Introduction

In April 1996, *The Council Chronicle* of the National Council of Teachers of English (NCTE) reported the results of a recent poll sponsored by *USA Today*, CNN, and Gallup. The poll showed that sixty-seven percent of citizens in the survey placed the quality of public education at the top of a list of concerns, followed in order by crime, the economy, availability of jobs, availability of heath insurance, health care costs, the national debt, drug abuse, and financial security for retirees (1). It's pretty obvious that a lot of people are concerned about schooling in the United States.

Students may be more concerned, or frustrated, than anyone else. Here's one illustration (we're sure you could supply your own). Our local newspaper in Norfolk, VA, *The Virginian-Pilot*, asked high school students this question, "If you could do one thing to improve education, what would it be?" The results appeared on October 13, 1995 (Friday the 13th, in fact). Hannah Bennett of Deep Creek High in Chesapeake, said, "More class discussion. You can read stuff out of the book and answer questions, but you never really learn it unless you talk about it" (E1). Hannah's fellow students, Kelly Bateman and Tanya Fiol, wanted to see more teacher enthusiasm. As Kelly put it, "I've had teachers who are great and they make you want to go to school and want to work to make good grades. It's not like that when the teacher doesn't have any enthusiasm" (E11). Nathaniel Reboja said, "Classes need to be more interactive. If you have classes involved in group activities, everyone has to participate. They have no choice" (E11). Actually, much of the research on effective teaching and learning is captured in these teenagers' comments:

> —*talking* and *writing* to *learn*—i.e., students using their own languages to produce questions and insights beyond the constraints of textbooks—teacher *enthusiasm*, the kind that *seduces* students to *want to*—want to be in school and want to do well there—classroom *interaction*—teacher-to-student, student-to-teacher, and student-to-student.

In classrooms defined by these qualities and conditions, students learn how to learn by creating meaning, by becoming intellectually absorbed in their work. They become readers and writers, not just students of reading and writing; historians, not just students of history; mathematicians, not just students of math; and so on. They become thirsty for ideas and information, for the skills to quench their thirst, and for thought-provoking questions that lead to insights that arouse them.

Yes, our profession has learned a lot about good teaching and good learning over the years, but schools can't seem to act on it across the board. One of the reasons for this failing is the natural human tendency to resist change, to point fingers at others, to fix blame elsewhere. We all do it. Yet, as Shakespeare knew when he gave these lines to Cassius in *Julius Caesar*, "The fault, dear Brutus, is not in our stars, but in ourselves, that we are underlings" (1925, 1. 2. 34). On we go, though, or as Ronald Reagan famously put it to Jimmy Carter, "There you go again." College professors blame the high schools for students falling short; high schools blame middle schools; middle schools blame elementary schools; elementary schools blame kindergartens; mothers blame fathers; and fathers may say, "Wait a minute! I'm not sure she's my kid anyway!" So nobody takes responsibility at any level of contact.

Because it's a natural human tendency (perhaps even need) to point fingers, permit us to do a little finger-pointing, as well. It's a way of expressing our own concerns, which led to this book. Specifically, what are we and others (probably you, too) concerned about? We're concerned about a system of schooling in the United States that hasn't changed much since we, ourselves, were children (even since our parents and their parents were children); concerned about the ever-widening gap between the world of school and the world that school is supposed to prepare all students for; concerned about critics who seem more bent on declaring open war on schools than on treating them as societal family members in need of nurturing and support; concerned about current school reform movements that treat teachers, at best, as well-meaning but second-rate semiprofessionals or, at worst, as imbeciles who cannot be trusted; and concerned about educational policymakers and bureaucrats who (from comfortable, distant offices and chairs) continue to employ top-down approaches to trying to improve the situation. (One of us used to be a bureaucrat with a State Department of Public Instruction. We often used to hear in those days the three classic lies, "The check is in the mail; I'll love you tomorrow like I love you tonight; and I'm from the State Department and I'm here to help you.") Now, with these concerns duly catalogued, let's turn to a little recent history.

In the late 1960s and 1970s there was a flurry of activity among so-called "romantic" critics of schools, serious professionals interested in revolutionizing the United States' system of education. They wanted to revolutionize because that's what romantics are driven to do. These were savvy, intense thinkers and writers from several academic disciplines within and without the field of education—people like Paul Goodman, Herbert Kohl, Carl Rogers, Jerome Bruner, John Gardner, Bob Samples, Robert Coles, Maxine Greene, John Holt, Nat Hentoff, Jonathan Kozol, Ivan Illich, and, specifically in English education, James Moffett, Louise Rosenblatt, Ken Macrorie, Daniel Fader, and Eliot Wigginton. Two of the most influential romantic school reformers of that period, whose work cuts across the general field of education, are Neil Postman and Charles Weingartner. Their *Teaching as a Subversive Activity* (1969) was a bright, brash, bold, fresh, witty, and shocking critique of schools, with an advocacy of a "new education" grounded in inquiry approaches to teaching and learning.

The two of us, writing this more than twenty-five years down the road from reading that remarkable book, can say that its impact on us as young English teachers at the time (one of us in the American North and the other in the American South) was profound. Postman and Weingartner described a school system floundering within an obsolete, conceptual model of the past, devoted to looking backward and oblivious to the future. They portrayed a school system staring "fixedly into the past as we hurtle pell-mell into the future" (216). They described what students did in classrooms of that time.

> Well, mostly they sit and listen to the teacher. Mostly, they are required to believe in authorities, or at least pretend to such belief when they take tests. Mostly, they are required to remember. They are almost never required to make observations, formulate definitions or perform any intellectual operations that go beyond repeating what someone else says is true. They are rarely encouraged to ask substantive questions, although they are permitted to ask about administrative and technical details. (How long should the paper be? Does spelling count? When is the assignment due?) It is practically unheard of for students to play any role in determining what problems are worth studying or what procedures of inquiry ought to be used. (19)

What did students learn in such school environments? Some of what they learned, according to Postman and Weingartner, includes the following:

> Passive acceptance is a more desirable response to ideas than active criticism. . . . Recall is the highest form of intellectual achievement, and the collection of unrelated "facts" is the goal of education. . . . One's own ideas and those of one's classmates are inconsequential.

. . . Feelings are irrelevant in education. . . . There is always a
single, unambiguous Right Answer to a question. . . (20–21).

Schools must change to a student-centered, inquiry-based model of
education, they declared: "The older school environments stressed
that learning is being told what happened. The inquiry environment
stresses that learning is a happening in itself" (29); and, ". . . the
new education, in addition to being student-centered and question-
centered, must also be language-centered" (102).

To many (we hope all) readers, what we have lifted from Postman and Weingartner seems old news. The criticism is now quite
familiar, and over the last twenty-five years or so, to be fair, the
ideas of the "new education" have taken hold in many schools and
classrooms across the United States. They are ideas that have won
the hearts and minds of many teachers, particularly English teachers. It's not as if no progress has been made. But there are still many,
both within and without the discipline of English education, who
continue to prepare students for a future based on certainty rather
than ambiguity, a future based on "fixed truths" rather than dynamic change, a future based on an industrial society rather than an
info-technical, entrepreneurial age. It is an age that requires the
ability to bob and weave, not just stand pat.

Ours is still a time, as Postman and Weingartner described nearly thirty years ago, in which many problems are unprecedented and
the demands of daily living are radically different from those of the
past. Clearly, schools have to catch up. No other alternative is a good
one. Yet, the ideas for change promoted by well-informed school
critics of the last three decades are currently under attack by many
citizens and educational policymakers. Many of the current attack-
ers blame so-called student-centered teaching (to let that phrase
stand a moment for the new education) for much of what's wrong
with schools today. They say such teaching coddles students, demands little of them, "waters down" the curriculum, encourages dis-
ruption, and leads to low achievement. The problem with fixing
blame in this direction is that *while the most thoughtful reform ideas
of the past have filled the literature on teaching and learning, they
most certainly have not filled the schools.* Many schools still operate
according to obsolete assumptions and old models, which may have
been adequate for other generations but not for the present and future age. Yet, many teachers—especially English teachers—have em-
braced the new education, and their students have benefited from
the embrace. It is the premise of this book that such teachers must
now *lead* school reform.

Our profession has learned a lot in the last forty years about teaching and learning, and we address many of these insights in this book. Mainly, however, we wish to link the beliefs, habits, behaviors, and best practices of English teachers to strategies for effective school reform. We want to challenge English teachers to help create *teacher*-centered as well as student-centered schools—that is, places where teachers think, talk, and work together to improve climates for teaching and learning, thereby increasing and targeting student achievement for the world outside of school, the world that exists now and that will continue to change at an accelerated pace. There's blame enough to go around. It's time to come together, and it's time for teachers to seize control of the direction for school change. It's time for teachers to seize control of their profession. For while the date is later (since 1969), the problems are much the same—they've changed, but they are still all too familiar.

In *Teaching as a Subversive Activity*, Postman and Weingartner spoke of many problems that schools have largely ignored, but three in particular:

1. the "communications revolution," or media change, referring to Father John Culkin of Fordham University saying that a lot of things have happened in this century and most of them plug into walls (6)
2. the "change revolution," pointing out that the nature of change has changed—it's faster (10)
3. the "burgeoning bureaucracy," saying that its function is to resist genuine change (12).

These problems are not only still around, they've heated up. Even more things plug into walls (or into surge protectors), change is faster still, and bureaucracies are still burgeoning, the Republican Contract with America notwithstanding. There is an even greater need for a new education than ever before. It's ironic that while we know what this new education is (person-centered, dialogue-oriented, and inquiry-dominated classroom communities), many schools cannot seem to apprehend it. It's like football teams fighting each other like crazy between the five yard lines and never able to cross the goal at either end.

Postman and Weingartner point out that mental illness, crime, and "the credibility gap" (which, they say, ". . . takes a variety of forms, such as lies, clichés, and rumors, and implicates almost everybody, including the President of the United States") are additional problems that, left unchecked, ". . . mean disaster for us and our children" (xi, xii). Walking down any street of any big U.S. city today is enough to convince anyone that the mental illness problem has gotten worse. The crime problem is clearly worse, (the United States' incarceration rate is currently greater than any other nation's on Earth, as syndicated columnist Molly Ivins noted during the Christmas season in "Welfare Reform Will Hurt Kids," *The Virginian Pilot*, December 29, 1995). President Clinton, as we write, is implicated in Whitewater and "Filegate" as President Johnson was in Vietnam and President Nixon was in Watergate during the 60s and 70s, respectively, blatantly illustrating that the credibility problem still afflicts us. What all of this means is this: if we want our schools fixed, *we're* going to have to fix them. And who are *we*? Those of us who are closest to them—teachers and students and others whose lives and livelihoods are most intimately entwined with them. Moreover, we believe that English teachers are the best equipped core-leadership group to turn school reform in a new, learner-focused direction.

A last word about *Teaching as a Subversive Activity* before we leave it. If you look up *subversive*, you find that one word used to define it is *corrupt*; if you look up *seductive*, you find the same word, *corrupt*, used to define it. Postman and Weingartner no more took *subversive* to mean *corrupt* than we now take *seductive* to mean *corrupt*. We believe, in these times, people must be seduced to subversion—that is, aroused, attracted, led, and won over to changing their life conditions and to doing better work. We mean to challenge English teachers, especially, to engage in this kind of seduction with students and colleagues to bring about needed school reform. When Thomas Paine wrote *The Crisis* (1776), he meant to call citizens to arms. He opened with this challenge:

> These are times that try men's souls. The summer soldier and the sunshine patriot will, in this crisis, shrink from the service of their country; but he that stands it now, deserves the love and thanks of man and woman. Tyranny, like hell, is not easily conquered; yet we have this consolation with us, that the harder the conflict, the more glorious the triumph. What we obtain too cheap, we esteem too lightly; 'tis dearness only that gives value (1).

But it is not battlelines we wish to draw, not militancy we wish to propose. We think teachers must work to bring themselves together, not split themselves asunder. As Voltaire (who died in France two years after the appearance of Paine's *The Crisis*) observed in his play *Merope*, through the character of Polyphonte, "It is not enough to conquer; one must learn to seduce" (1925, I. 4. 306)—to lead, attract, win over. Schools must become more seductive places, in large part because the street world outside of schools is *too* seductive. And in the competition for students' lives, in far too many cases the streets are winning.

In Chapter One we offer an extended rationale for our use of the word *seductive*, and we explain more fully why we think seductive English teachers are the natural leaders of school reform. In Chapter Two we discuss two problems that English teachers as school reformers must lead schools toward solving—problems that affect everyone—the *violence* problem and the *literacy* problem. We contrast an idyllic picture of schools that many adults claim to remember (the old order) with a current view of schools as stark and depressing places on the brink of chaos (the new order). Reform efforts that slight the violence and literary problems, choosing instead to focus superficially on competitive test scores, are merely "moving deck chairs around on the *Titanic*." Chapter Three identifies the National Writing Project as a model for school reform, the kind of deep and broad school improvement that only teachers can bring about. It is a bottom-up rather than a top-down model, and the two of us have been affiliated with it for nearly twenty years. Reform is at its best when teachers are viewed as reformers rather than reformees, as the National Writing Project acknowledges.

When English teachers work as school reformers, they encounter two critical factors in leading both students and colleagues to do better work: one is the "subject/object" factor and the other is the "self-efficacy/environment-building" factor. We treat these respectively in Chapters Four and Five. The subject/object factor (Chapter Four) has to do with how one views the act of teaching, learning, and growing. English teachers, largely because of the discipline they teach, know perhaps better than anyone else the importance of integrating the subjective view—offering hope, freedom, encouragement to take risks, spontaneity, and vision—with the "objective" view—insisting upon diligence, order, maintenance, rigor, and discipline. Resolving this tension is necessary to both learning well and teaching well, not to mention bringing about needed school reform. One significant job of English teachers as school reformers is to *raise the level of thinking and talking about teaching and learning in their schools*. Self-efficacy and environment-building (Chapter Five) has to do with creating classroom and whole-school climates that are hospitable to raising that level of thought and discussion. Seductive English teachers help to build language-rich environments that make strong, give-and-take relationships possible and that increase everyone's sense of self-efficacy—students' and colleagues' alike—by reaching high. The last chapter (Chapter Six) offers our own theory of teacher growth and tries to answer the question, "How does one become a master practitioner and leader among both students and colleagues?" We include a set of modest proposals that English teachers might consider for their own schools to change things for the better.

We've saved the last problem we wish to identify here until this last paragraph, although it is implied in much of what we have already ranted about. It's the problem of obstacles to school reform, and there are two classifications we have in mind. One is ideas. The educational establishment is certainly not short of ideas to make schools better, but some ideas will work and others won't help at all. The ones that won't help are an obstacle. The other obstacle is people, and this one must be addressed with emphasis. The people factor is why seduction is necessary. *People in our time must be aroused and led to find the courage, the energy, the time, the wisdom, and the will to make schools right, really right.* It's not that some people want better schools and some don't. It's a question of who should be playing what roles in the process of improving them. Our position is that tangible, visible, and substantial school reform depends on teachers, not as mere conduits for outsiders' ideas, but as shapers of reform that actually helps everyone do better work in school. Across these pages you'll meet teachers and students who are doing that job. We need more of them. Their numbers will increase when outstanding teachers *decide to lead* and to accept the challenge of directing school reform. We trust this book might further the effort.

References

de Voltaire, Marie Francois Arrouet. 1925. *Merope*, ed. Thomas Edward Oliver. New York, NY: The Century Company.

"Election-Year Focus on Education May Do More Harm than Good." 1996. *The Council Chronicle*, April.

"If You Could Do One Thing to Improve Education, What Would It Be?" 1995. *The Virginian-Pilot*, 13 October.

Ivins, Molly. 1995. "Welfare Reform Will Hurt Kids." *The Virginian-Pilot*, 29 December.

Paine, Thomas. 1968. *The Crisis*. In *American Literature*, ed. Mark Schorer, et al. 165–168. New York, NY: Houghton Mifflin.

Postman, Neil, and Weingartner, Charles. 1969. *Teaching as a Subversive Activity*. New York, NY: Dell.

Shakespeare, William. 1925. *Julius Caesar*. In *Complete Works*. New York, NY: P. F. Collier and Son.

Chapter One

Seductive Teaching
(English and Otherwise)
What It Is and Why We Need It

Since this book is about teaching, we'll start with some questions. If you answer honestly, give yourself an A⁺. Here goes.

1. Do you have a loving relationship with someone other than a blood relative?
2. Do you live with another person?
3. Do you have one or more children?
4. Do you like stories—like to hear them, read them, and tell them?
5. Do you like to talk and write about books or films that move you?
6. Have you ever helped anyone do anything, just because you want to?
7. Have you ever won an argument?
8. Does anyone (besides, perhaps, yourself) consider you to be an uncommonly good listener?
9. Do you have a job in which one or more people "report" to you?
10. Are there people who see you as a leader?

If you answered "yes" to any of these questions, you may be a teacher, although you might not get paid (enough, anyway) for the teaching you do. If you answered "yes" to 1, 7, 8, and 10, there's a good chance you're a *seductive* teacher, at least potentially. If you answered "yes" to 1, 4, 5, 7, 8, and 10, you are likely a seductive English teacher or well on your way to becoming one.

In the broadest sense, everyone's a teacher. Teaching is a natural act of caring, driven by the need to protect a species. Creatures have always nurtured their young by helping them survive and become independent, eventually able to fend for themselves and to teach their offspring to do the same. When the first human being on earth encountered the second, teaching as we know it began.

Teaching is arguably the noblest and certainly one of the oldest of human activities. Without it, our species would be dead by now. Teaching spread the languages we use, the science we believe in, the arts we appreciate, the values we hold, and the cultures we embrace. It is responsible in large measure for all we are and might become because to teach well is to arouse, to attract, to lead.

Everyone teaches someone some time, often without seeming to. Children watch adults—parents and others—and learn from them. Until we go to school, teaching tends to be indirect and informal. School turns it all around. School makes teaching direct and formal because teaching is the school's "business."

It follows, then, that in a ideal world, only the best teachers would be tapped to work in schools. In schools, teaching is (or ought to be) a profession. Some of us are better teachers than others, of course. Some have a knack for teaching, as others have knacks for other things. Yet, as both an art and a science, teaching is an activity we can all learn to do better. Who are the best teachers among us, and how do we recognize them? How can the rest of us improve at this universal job? This book addresses such questions. Our introductory, first-blush answer is that to be a superb teacher, one must possess seductive powers. This is a crucial factor. Some of us possess such powers naturally, but *all* of us can acquire and develop them more fully.

Seductive is a word that often suggests the sinister or the suspicious, as in "Playing the seductive con man, Adam charmed his victims out of all their possessions." *The Random House Dictionary of the English Language* gives the first definition for *seduce* as, "to lead astray . . . corrupt"; the second definition, "to persuade or induce to have sexual intercourse"; and the third, "to . . . draw away, as from principles, faith, or allegiance" (1987, 1732).

Let us be quick to say that we mean none of these things in our use of *seduce* and *seductive* in this chapter. Since we believe that good and thoughtful readers tend to re-read, we invite you to re-read the previous sentence. Since we can't be sure you did, we will repeat it. *We mean none of these things in our use of seduce and seductive in this chapter.*

Fortunately for us, the fourth definition our dictionary gives for *seduce* is "to win over; attract. . . . " From Latin, *ducere* means "to lead." It's in these three senses that we use *seduce* and *seductive*—*win over, attract,* and *lead.* Seductive teachers are able to win over, attract, and lead their students and colleagues. That's what we mean by "seductive teaching." Further, because teaching leans heavily upon powers of communication, we believe English teachers are potentially the best resources for helping others teach seductively. That's why they must become leaders of school reform. Sensible school reform, like good teaching itself, demands seductive activity. Much of the rhetoric of reform has been strident, and some educational reformers have treated schools and teachers almost as enemies of substantial progress, not as partners. Useful reform will not draw battlelines between schools and school critics. Remember Voltaire's dictum (from our introduction, unless you skipped it), "It is not enough to conquer; one must learn to seduce." Or, as Kurt Vonnegut observes in *Palm Sunday*, "It is this genuine caring, and not your games with language, which will be the most compelling and seductive element in your style" (1981, 77). (Although Vonnegut is discussing the craft of writing here, he might also have been commenting on the craft of teaching.)

Seductive teachers "sell" students on the learning opportunities that school provides. They win over students and attract them to seeing their classrooms as safe havens that can nurture their growth. Many students, increasing in number, need to be sold on this vision. Seductive English teachers can win over their colleagues to a similar vision; that is, teachers and administrators working cooperatively in environments that nurture *their* growth, as well. By extolling and practicing virtues inherent in the humanities—and in their well-honed pedagogical processes—teachers can help build such working environments. They can help build dynamic schools in which dissenting voices are heard, valued, respected, and considered. In such places, people grow and conditions improve for everyone. School reform flourishes. In such schools, teachers have decided to lead.

When we speak of seductive teachers leading school reform, we obviously do not mean leading astray, as in the more devious use of *seduce.* We do not mean that such teachers lead students through rigid routes of learning to which all must conform. What we *do* mean is that seductive teachers lead students toward finding their own learning routes that make them strong and able human beings—people who know how to learn, who care about learning, who can cope with change, and who can contribute productively to a democratic society. English teachers can lead their colleagues along the same routes.

English teachers enable students to develop literacy (reading and writing ability) and oracy (speaking and listening ability). In doing so, they enable students to succeed in all other areas of the school curriculum, as well. But good teachers know they cannot accomplish these things *for* students. They know students must learn *for themselves*. They know that a successful school is not a place where young people come to watch old people work, or where some teachers work less and less well than others. A successful school is not a place for slackers, at any age.

Schools must be places where young people come to work with older people who can help them want to be there too, and who can genuinely help them succeed. Seductive teachers know that their first job is to have students see school in this way. The rewards, however, may not be immediate. As William Glasser, noted school reformer, observes in *The Quality School*, ". . . a teacher may do a good job all year and *sell* her class on the value of quality work, but the payoff...may not be obvious until the following year" (1990, 20). Seductive English teachers inspire their colleagues in the same ways that they inspire students. Such teachers realize that not all of their colleagues will conform to the same approaches to teaching and working with kids, that their colleagues must find their own ways of achieving success, and that their colleagues must learn for themselves what works best. But seductive English teachers can help create school climates that foster both student and teacher growth, that value diversity and divergence, and that promote mutual respect. In such a climate, everyone wins.

In a *New York Times* article on May 22, 1994, with the lead "The Huffingtons of Washington believe that social revolution begins at home," reporter Karen De Witt describes a practice by Congressman Michael Huffington and his wife of hosting dinner parties for people they don't really know. Unique in that fact alone, these dinner parties have another special twist. Their purpose is to bring together people of common interest and expertise to discuss specific topics of national, even global, importance: health care, volunteerism, racism, spirituality, and the like. Mrs. Huffington says that the couple's quest is to discover "how to seduce people into doing good" (4). (Regardless of how we or you feel about the Huffingtons' political or personal persuasions, it is in a similar vein that we use the word *seductive*: to explain how some teachers are able to urge students and colleagues "into doing good"—good for themselves as learners and good for a democratic society).

We also want to dispel a common view about teachers today, a view that too many people hold. Holden Caulfield, the adolescent rebel in J. D. Salinger's *The Catcher in the Rye*, illustrates this view bluntly, "It's funny. You don't have to think too hard when you talk to a teacher" (1945, 13). We don't think that's "funny" at all. We want to show that seductive teachers do in fact require students "to think hard." They also inspire their colleagues "to think hard." But how do seductive teachers do that? A lot depends upon relationships they build with both.

In *New Arabian Nights*, Robert Louis Stevenson wrote, "The Prince . . . gained the affection of all classes by the seduction of his manner" (1894, 7). If we change Stevenson's word *Prince* to *Teacher*, we move toward capturing a fuller sense of what we mean by seductive. The seductive teacher, like Stevenson's prince, gains "the affection of all classes" of students, regardless of their color, gender, race, or economic circumstance. We deal in later chapters with how seductive teachers think, feel, perceive their worlds, relate to students and colleagues, and otherwise behave. We will elaborate on how one becomes such a teacher. For now, though, we wish to offer just a basic sketch.

In *Tess of the D'Urbervilles* (1891), Thomas Hardy says of Tess, "One reason why she seduces casual attention is that she never courts it" (1972, 82). Like Tess, seductive teachers seduce subtly. They are more indirect than direct; they lead by example; they "show" more than they "tell"; they get what they want (respect, courteous treatment, enthusiasm, hard work) by giving students and colleagues the same; they expect a lot, so they get a lot, too. In the words of the late Jim Valvano, coach of the North Carolina State University national championship basketball team in 1983, they "never give up." Now what might amaze some people is this: there are many, many of these teachers out there in our schools. There are also many more who wish to join—indeed, are capable of joining—their ranks.

Seductive teachers may or may not teach in seductive schools. Some schools—granted, too few—are hospitable to such teachers who work in them and to kids who attend them. Such schools do exist, much public and media opinion to the contrary. Given what we see on television and read in the print media nowadays, it may be easy to believe that *no* seductive schools exist, at least in the public sector. But they do. They're there. If you're a seductive teacher in a seductive school, your job is still hard but not as hard. You work with a safety net and a support system that allow you to take risks and that encourage innovation. You reach high and, often, students—colleagues, as well—respond in remarkable ways.

Many more seductive teachers work in schools that are not particularly so. In this case, the teacher's job is more difficult. Every school is but a reflection of the complex cultural character that defines the community it serves. Even in nonseductive schools, however, seductive teachers still have faith—naive to some—that their classrooms belong mutually to them and their students, and when the doors of those classrooms are closed, with only the kids and teachers present, a separate world exists. This world has the potential to become magical. Seductive teachers know that magic will occur if magic is allowed; they create opportunities that allow the magic. They do so by building learning environments that are safe and that kids help to shape and protect because they, too, are shareholders in these environments.

Seductive teachers, however, are neither miracle workers nor wizards. They are people with the same foibles, fears, and shortcomings of other people, but they know that seduction ultimately fails if it is not gradual and genuine. All good teachers know that the first days and weeks of any school year are crucial to determining the success or failure of their efforts to seduce students into states of *learning pleasure*. Such teachers know that to seduce their students truly—win them over, attract them, lead them—is a slow and gradual process with many starts, stops, and changes of pace. So from the first day of school, good teachers begin this slow and gradual process of drawing students in and of drawing them out. They know that winning students over, attracting them, and leading them take uncommon energy and lots of time. The result, though, is worth the effort, especially when students begin to demonstrate that they truly value schooling as important to their lives.

Students are drawn to seductive teachers; they appreciate the energy, time, and care such teachers give them. These teachers are memorable, and their influence runs deep, as the following case illustrates. Nelson Lopez is in his late thirties. He's in college studying to become a high school math teacher. He remembers a teacher who made him believe in himself, who made him believe he could learn. Nelson is Puerto Rican, and English is his second language. With his mother, father, and six brothers, he grew up in Harlem and in Bethlehem, Pennsylvania. During those years his family lived in apartments in which his father worked as a building superintendent. As Nelson says,

In one building, we lived in the basement. We all pitched in to help my dad. We always took out the trash, maybe a hundred cans daily. We helped with painting, fixing, and cleaning up. I can see how people look down on this type of people, but we were never the type to look down on. My mom and dad gave me a lot of love. Usually we got a better apartment. Sometimes my dad would have two buildings where he had workers under him to help. English was my second language, but I didn't even realize this until maybe my teens. I didn't learn English at home. I learned Spanish. If my mom walked in here right now, English would leave my head and Spanish would come in. I learned English from my older brothers, who learned it in the streets.

Growing up, Nelson Lopez went to many schools but never learned to read and write English very well. He explains,

I went to Vo-Tech in the ninth grade because nobody thought I was college material. Somebody must have said, "This kid is not college bound so stick him over here." Nobody asked me, so I'm off to Vo-Tech. But I liked it. It was a big plus for me at the time. My mom would go, "You can learn a trade and become a carpenter." I thought, I'm not going to be rich and famous, so why not? Everything there was hands on, little instruction. They gave you a piece of wood, showed you how to cut it, and you cut it. I always thought everything I did wasn't good enough, but I started getting A's there and I said, "Hey, this is cool." I got straight A's in my junior and senior years, but I graduated without having to read or write much.

Nelson talks about working as a painter during his years in trade school. When more jobs began to come his way, he began hiring others to work with him. He began making money and feeling good.

I said, "Hey, this is all right," and I was actually starting to think that maybe I'm not stupid. There was always a struggle with this. I couldn't write and read, but I worked in painting and carpentry and got into that. But I struggled with manuals. I could usually get by just looking at the pictures. My confidence was building because I was working and making money—doing well—no reading and writing involved. But as I got more successful, I had to write checks—kind of scary. How do I punctuate? Is it September-comma-1-year or September-1-comma-year? I didn't know. I felt more frustration when I had to make bids on jobs. And people would ask me for receipts. I would freeze. I'd say, "Don't you get your checks back? Can't those be your receipts?" But I knew I had to stop faking it.

So Nelson went to Allentown College just to learn how to read and write. He'd heard about a special program there, in his words, "for predominantly poor kids who had my problem." On his first visit he met Margaret Bilheimer. Here is how he came to regard her.

> I actually started realizing you can learn because somebody believed in you. Somebody encouraged you. Somebody really believed in me more than I believed in me. Ms. Bilheimer won me over right away, and she was so friendly. I couldn't understand that. She got my attention. She asked about *me*. One of the biggest things I learned from her was how to find out what I needed to know—in books, from people, and other sources. "Go get this book," she would say, "and I'll help you with it.' . . . "You're kidding me," I thought. But I'm not the type that won't work for something once I see a reason. I'll work really hard when I get excited. That's why lazy teachers tick me off.

Nelson Lopez speaks eloquently with high animation about his teacher who opened doors to literacy for him.

> I liked her. I love her 'till today. The first thing I'm going to do when I graduate is go back there and give her a big hug and kiss. She'll fight for any poor kid. She did more for me than just teaching. She brought to me a feeling that I could do anything. She'd say, "Nelson, you can do more than just barely make it." She'd say, "Think about what you want to write." She was the first to say that to me. I was excited. That's all it took. "What do you want to write?" And I said, "Fine. Painting and having my own business and my brothers and wrestling." But I asked, "Don't I have to have some rules? Don't I need to know how long?" "No," she said. "Just write. The rules will come in due time." I thought, "Yes, but what if it's a failure?" Everything had been so negative. She said, "Look. You're going to write the paper, I'm going to look at it, talk with you about it, and you're going to write it again." "You mean you're going to give me a second chance after I mess up the first time? I've never had second chances." It's like, wow. I'm thinking she's weird now. So now I'm enjoying it instead of fighting it. So I would write and she would ask questions. Like, "What are you saying here? Read this sentence to me. Why do you say it this way! What other words can you use? Can you be more specific? Can you think of synonyms?" I found out what a synonym was! She told me about *Roget's Thesaurus*. I thought, "Wow, you mean they've got books that can do this?" I was naive. Every time I was with her, I'd get excited. I get excited talking about it now.

Ms. Bilheimer helped Nelson in other ways, too, not just with reading and writing. She helped him acquire a can-do attitude, a sense of self-efficacy, a set of personal standards and qualities that go with achievement of any significant kind. Here are his final comments.

Ms. Bilheimer gave a lot of encouragement. She said, "You can't quit. You have great *potential*." I'd say, "What's that?" And she'd say, "Look it up," and I would. She showed me there are places to find anything you really need to know. I saved my papers I wrote for her. This was fifteen or so years ago and I still have them at home some place. They were that special to me. They were short papers, maybe a paragraph or two. I thought, "That's all you want? You don't want ten pages typed and all that stuff? Wow!" She went beyond teaching to make sure I succeeded. When you got stuck, she'd help you. Some kids were more stuck than others. I was probably one of the most stuck. But I honestly felt I had potential because she told me I did. I'd say, "Are you serious?" And she'd say, "Yes." I was believing it. She might have used the same line to every single student there, I don't know. But I was feeling like I could do it, I could do it—instead of "I'm stupid, I'm stupid." I was getting in my head that I could do it. Oh, another thing she used to tell me was, "You have to be tenacious!" *Tenacious*, what did that mean? And, of course, she would say, "Look it up!" She was sincere. She wasn't faking it. It wasn't a job to her. She worked so hard trying to make me learn, and you knew if she was working that hard, you could do it, too. And the other word she made me learn was *intimidate*. She would say, "Don't let anything intimidate you." She always made time for me. She led me. I don't feel, as a lot of teachers seem to, that leading and helping is bad. Her expectations of me were probably higher than anybody's. At first, I was like, "This lady is strange." Not in a bad way, in a good way. But she was interested and concerned. She got me excited. In the beginning, I believed in her, really, more than in myself. But then I thought, "If Ms. Bilheimer believes in me, I'm going to try." If I ever give up, I'll make a liar out of her. I don't want to make a liar out of her.

We can summarize the qualities of Nelson Lopez's teacher in this way. In his own words, he says she

- believed in me more than I believed in me
- won me over
- was so friendly
- got my attention
- asked about me
- taught me how to find out what I needed to know
- excited me
- brought to me a feeling that I could do anything
- gave a lot of encouragement
- (told him) "You can't quit. You have great potential"

- went beyond teaching to make sure I succeeded
- (told him) "You have to be tenacious"
- (told him) "Don't let anything intimidate you"
- always made time for me
- led me

Ms. Bilheimer obviously knew her stuff. But more, she knew how to communicate with students like Nelson Lopez. Now Nelson wants to be a teacher.

What do seductive teachers do in classrooms—middle and high school classrooms—that attract students, lead them, and win them over to doing high-quality work? Here's an example. As we write this, Beth Bond is in her fifth year of teaching English at Tallwood High School in Virginia Beach, Virginia. As her twelfth-grade students approach their classroom on this October day, they see a sign on the door that reads "Museum Entrance." Beth is standing at the door, greeting students and collecting their "Museum Passes," which she gave them the day before. To obtain entrance today, students have written their responses on these "passes" to the question, "Who Am I?" As students look around the room, they see art work all over the walls—Miro's "Women, Bird, and Star," Dali's "The Birth of Liquid Desires," Picasso's "The Couple," Magritte's "The Surprise Answer," Chagall's "The Fall of the Angel" (a student looks at this one and says, "The guy who drew this needs some medicine!"), De Chirico's "The Endless Voyage," and so on. Beth tells the class, "Walk around the room and look at these pieces of art. Think of words that describe what you see. Mainly, I want you to see what connections you can make between what you're seeing today and what you've been reading." What students have been reading in this heterogeneous English class are Camus' *The Stranger*, Beckett's *Waiting for Godot*, and Kafka's *The Metamorphosis*. Each student is reading one of these books and working with a small group of other students who are also reading it. Eventually, there will be three small-group presentations to the class on the books—one book per group. Each group will decide how it will make its presentation.

Next, Beth says, "O.K., travel back to your seats now, and let's discuss the connections you're making." After some conversation with students about the art work and the books, Beth announces that she will now play two songs by the rock groups Collective Soul ("Scream") and REM ("Losing My Religion"). She also gives students a handout of the lyrics. She says, "As you listen to these songs, try to pick one line from each that reminds you in some way of a character you've been reading about, and be prepared to say why." During the ensuing discussion, nearly all students have something to say in this culturally plural, ethnically mixed class. Beth listens attentively to their responses, encouraging and pressing each student to say more, to think ever more deeply. She asks many follow-up questions to students' initial responses. It is clear that hers is a response-centered English class, in which a teacher and students regularly interrogate texts and each other to make meanings.

Finally, Beth says, "You needed a pass to get into class today; you need one to get out, too. I'm going to pass out 'exit slips,' and you have ten minutes to write on them an answer to the question 'Why are we here'? Think of the art prints you've seen, the music you've heard, and the books you're reading as you answer this question." Students get down to work. Beth stands at the door and cheerfully collects "exit slips" as students move out into the hall.

Another fifty-minute class has ended in this teacher's classroom in which the teacher is planner, guide, researcher, and innovator and the students are workers. Capitalizing on their multiple intelligences, Beth Bond is *leading, attracting,* and *winning over* students to the humanities—making connections between their own lives and those of characters in the painting, music and literature they study. In the process, students are learning to read, write, speak, listen, view, and think critically and imaginatively. It's a gradual process, not a "quick fix." Of course, not every day is Beth Bond's classroom a museum. Some days it may be a studio, a workshop, a theater, a technology center, a conference room, a library, a laboratory, a lecture hall, a discussion circle, or combinations thereof. Not every day's work is a teaching and learning masterpiece, but her classroom is always a place that *invites* learning, a place where students can take risks, challenge and be challenged, and be led to do high-quality work. Seductive teachers do what works, and they vary their approaches to doing so. For them, the conduct of the classroom is not just business-as-usual, not just routine, not just formulaic. The atmosphere is filled with a healthy learning tension.

Teaching seductively is not like buying (or selling) a fast-food hamburger. We've had too much of the fast-food approach to educating students in the past several decades. We've had too many packaged programs, formulas, step-by-step methodologies and materials, slogans (*a mind is a terrible thing to waste; just say no; do more with less*—as if such sound bites can actually change things), curriculum revisions, testing programs, one-shot teacher workshops in late afternoons, blue ribbon committees to develop standards, and other not-so-grand plans and designs. We've had too few seductive teachers.

We've lost sight of the fact that it is not any of the items above that will significantly increase and improve student learning; it is the teacher who must do that, if it is to be done at all. As *Time* magazine writer Claudis Wallis has observed, "Fifty years of top-down reform have not done the trick" (1994, 55). Regardless of anything negative in their lives, if kids encounter one truly seductive teacher, their lives can be transformed, as in the case of Nelson Lopez. Throughout history, there are too many grown-up, successful human beings—many from dire and humble beginnings—who have testified to that fact for it to be seriously disputed. If going back to basics is indeed a viable way to improve schooling, the "basics" represented by the following are the ones to go back to.

For example, in his address to Williams College alumni in New York, President James Abram Garfield declared in this well-worn passage,

> I am not willing that this discussion should close without mention of the value of a true teacher. Give me a log hut, with only a simple bench, Mark Hopkins on one end and I on the other, and you may have all the buildings, apparatus and libraries without him (Hinsdale 1882, 43).

(Mark Hopkins was president of Williams College at the time of this address, which was extemporaneous and never formally recorded, the words "remembered" and passed on by those present.) Garfield's impassioned point reintroduces what we have already implied: more than anything else—length of the school day and year, school facilities, students in uniforms and separated by gender, instructional equipment and materials, streamlined curricula, standardized assessments, or other trappings of so-called school reform—it is the teacher who counts most, who makes whatever lasting difference is to be made.

As Henry Adams noted in another famous statement, from *The Education of Henry Adams*, "A teacher affects eternity; he can never tell where his influence stops" (1931, 43). *Influence* is a propitious word here. Its original meaning, as Chaucer uses it in *The Canterbury Tales*, was an ethereal fluid from the stars that penetrated a baby's body at birth and determined its destiny. Seductive teachers have at least an intuitive sense that their effects on students can indeed be that potent. Their effects on colleagues can be equally so.

According to his biographer Harvey Cushing, Sir William Osler, influential British educator of the nineteenth century, was reputed to have said, "No bubble is so iridescent or floats longer than that blown by the successful teacher" (1925, 295–296). Johann Wolfgang

Von Goethe wrote in *Elective Affinities* (1808), as translated by Mayer and Bogan, "A teacher who can arouse a feeling for one single good action, for one single good poem, accomplishes more than he who fills our memory with rows on rows of natural objects, classified with name and form" (1963, 214).

It is Goethe's observation, particularly, that begins to separate seductive teachers from other teachers. Some teachers behave as if education means merely filling the memory, day in and day out, "with rows on rows" of whatever the curriculum "contains"—put another way, a kind of gas-station approach to teaching. In such teachers' classrooms are kids who know this approach well. It may also be called the "empty vessel" approach, or *tabula rasa*, in John Locke's terms. In this context, the learner is a vessel—or gas tank, to stay with our more pedestrian metaphor—and the teacher is the service station attendant. When the bell rings, the teacher squeezes the trigger, and here comes the fuel. One (certainly not the only) problem with this approach is that kids who have pulled into the station have tanks with different capacities of need, even desire. Some are empty and would rather not take any fuel today, some are about half full, others are spilling over already, and so on.

The teacher as service station attendant pays little attention to this deep-structure phenomenon, however, and keeps holding the trigger and pumping the gas (never priming) until the bell rings again. At the sound of the second bell, there's fuel all over the place—same octane for all—and everybody (including the teacher) slips, slides, and runs over everybody else to get out of there before the whole room either ex- or implodes. It is this "model" of teaching that has been entrenched in our schools for a very long time, and—if you can believe this—it is what some of our fellow citizens yearn for when they call for a "return to rigor" or "back to basics." These are not basics to go back to. It's as if, when something goes wrong with the car, we want to go back to the horse and buggy. The world's a funny place sometimes.

There also are teachers who, having both felt and heard the effects of the gas-station approach, look around for other ways of "doing business" in their classrooms. Perhaps they go to a conference or workshop, they read an article in a professional journal, they hear an inspirational speaker, they listen to a "professional tape" in their automobile cassette players, they have available to them some "new" instructional technology and/or materials, or they read a threatening memorandum from school administrators about the need to prepare students better for state-wide tests. Like the gas station attendants, these teachers are good people, too. They want to do the right thing—they want their students to learn, and they want them to pass all the corporate tests they must take. So— and here is where the hope turns sour—they begin to try things in their classrooms that they don't fully grasp, or that represent a desperate groping to "just try something different."

Yet in the end, these new and promising ways prove disappointing, too. To be fair, they may have worked if

1. They were employed in a timely and judicious manner (after all, they were not invented by stupid people).

2. Teachers understood them fully and deeply and were committed to them.

3. They were given enough time for both teachers and kids to acquire the skill to do/use/manage them in order to make them work.

4. Perhaps most importantly, if teachers were connected on a daily basis with a seductive colleague, who could help when things go wrong.

A useful illustration of the "new ways" or "faddish" approach, which too often suffers and ultimately succumbs to impatience and superficiality (the fast-food syndrome again), comes from the movie *Teachers* (1984), starring Nick Nolte as a struggling, seductive teacher in a nonseductive school. A colleague of Nolte's character is another teacher called Mr. Ditto. Now Mr. Ditto is a good human being who wants to do the right thing by his students. We don't know for sure, but we might infer that Mr. Ditto was once a gas station–type teacher. He saw that this approach wasn't working. He had high absentee rates; he had discipline problems; his kids were failing tests; there was gas all over the floor after each period and little in students' tanks. They seemed to take less and less with each refueling, in fact.

Then (it is possible) he went to a late afternoon workshop, fairly early in his career, called "Individualizing Instruction through Programmed Materials," maybe in the early 1970s. While there, he heard the charismatic workshop leader, employed by a large textbook company, say something that became his motto forever, "Only the learner can do the learning; no one else can do it for him" (*him*—remember, it was the early 70s). That statement had the ring of truth for Mr. Ditto (as it does for good teachers everywhere). So he jumped on the bandwagon. He started Individualizing Instruction through Programmed Materials. The kids came in every day and went to work, silently in their seats.

The first year of this approach, Mr. Ditto actually walked among his students to monitor their progress and to help when asked. Then he began to sit at his desk more and more often, especially when attendance began to tail off again, and each year he still had the same categories of students, regardless of the differences in faces and names—those who achieved, those who barely squeaked by, and those who failed and became lost. The groups of failures seemed to be increasing, so Mr. Ditto decided to change again, though not much. He started creating his own worksheets for students to fill out in his classes, modeled after the "programmed materials" he had used (too expensive anyway), and he gave students tasks to do that he knew they *could* do. They still missed class a lot, but their test scores on his tests improved. After all, Mr. Ditto gave tests that were even easier than his worksheets, and students really didn't have to come to class much to pass the tests Mr. Ditto made. He also moved his desk to the back of the room so he would never have to face his students.

This scenario seemed to satisfy Mr. Ditto, finally, for he had lowered his expectations, and students seemed to be less tense. (Mr. Ditto never learned that a healthy amount of learning tension in a classroom is a desirable condition.) Pretty soon he was assigned to teach only remedial students, mainly because the super-concerned and involved parents of the high-achieving students claimed their kids weren't "doing much" in Mr. Ditto's classes. His worksheets kept the remedial students relatively quiet—numb, really; he had few discipline problems; his students passed his tests (O.K., they did less well on the standardized variety); he counted his days until retirement, and now he felt he could actually last that long. Then one fateful day—and this part *is* in the movie—Mr. Ditto slumped at his desk, sitting in his chair, face hidden by a newspaper. Two classes came and went, worksheets completed and left behind, before anyone noticed that Mr. Ditto was dead. Mr. Ditto died in his classroom as he had lived in his school—isolated from students and colleagues alike. Just one seductive teacher, interested in genuine educational reform and deciding to lead, might have changed Mr. Ditto's fate.

Not an uplifting little drama, we grant you. Exaggerated? Maybe. But scenes and situations not so different from this one play themselves out in schools across America each year. Frustration is the current name of the game, and everyone feels it—school boards, administrators, teachers, parents, and students alike.

So what can be done to improve things? There's a story about a school superintendent addressing a finance committee of a state legislature about his school district's desperate need for additional funds. When he had finished his plea, a senator responded explosively with, "Every year you people come here and beg for more money, money, money, money! I know you've got a problem, but we just can't keep throwing money at it!" To which the beleaguered but wary superintendent sighed, "Well, Senator, we've tried everything else. I thought we might give money a chance."

Of course, both the superintendent and the senator are right. States do not have bottomless pits of money, and schools need more than they currently have to make substantial changes—higher teacher salaries, reductions in class size and course loads, more and better instructional technology, greater per pupil expenditures, more opportunities for continuous faculty development, more school buildings and renovations of old ones. The list could drone on. We are not about to join the chorus of critics who argue that none of the items in our above list is particularly relevant to improving things. They clearly *are* relevant. More money *is* a necessary part of the solution to schools' problems, and to spend it on such items as we have listed would be a help, certainly not a waste.

We also, however, hold another view. On nation can spend its money on education far more wisely. While we do not intend to criticize or to snub any efforts to increase school funding, we do believe there is a solution just as fundamental to deep and lasting school improvement. That solution—as by now you might have guessed—is to fill schools with armies of seductive teachers. No additional funding for anything or everything else will have a substantial impact without a critical mass of such teachers in our schools. Writing in *Phi Delta Kappan*, Martin Haberman, Distinguished Professor of curriculum and instruction at the University of Wisconsin, Milwaukee, says, "I believe that one useful reform would be to increase the numbers of good teachers in second- and third-rate schools, so that all children have at least one teacher (out of more than 50 in 12 years) who cares about them and teaches them important ideas and ideals" (1994, 692). We do not wish to state the matter quite so cynically, nor to support the labeling of schools as first-rate, second-rate, and third-rate; however, simply put, to improve student learning, schools—all schools—can improve teaching. That's at least one "true" solution to a complex problem. If infusions of funds can help with that, be *focused* upon that, then we are fanatical supporters of such infusions and would gladly contribute our tax dollars to them.

If we were Kings of Education, we would most certainly refocus school funding, even increase it. But we would do so to increase the numbers of seductive teachers and clear the paths for them to build seductive learning environments for their students—this before anything else. President William Clinton and the United States Congress have concluded that a way to fight crime in America is to increase the numbers of police officers on city streets. If this is a good formula—and statistical data suggest that it is in places where it has been tried, like Nashville, Tennessee—a similar solution would also work in schools: more teachers—*seductive* teachers—equal school improvement. Reducing the student-teacher ratio to a maximum of fifteen to one—kindergarten through grade twelve—would be a huge help, a major step toward the kind of school reform our country truly needs. A seductive English teacher with sixty student essays to read will be more effective than one with a hundred-plus essays to read, to state the obvious. Moreover, Valerie E. Lee of the University of Michigan and Julia B. Smith of the University of Rochester have found in their research, reported in *The Virginian-Pilot*, April 14, 1996: . . . "schools with 600 to 900 students are the most optimal for learning" (J4). How educational policymakers target and increase available funds to improve schooling is a crucial issue. Spending money to make schools *smaller* is a good idea, a useful policy/funding/administrative reform idea.

We're not saying merely that schools need better teachers, for that's too easy and vague to say. Better how? Taller? Smarter? Younger? More aggressive? More docile? More political? More tactful? More liberal? More conservative? Quicker on the draw? No, what schools need are well-paid, seductive teachers and more of them, with fewer students to teach. Further, a major premise of this book is that English teachers, through administrative policies that encourage and invite them to work as consultants to their colleagues, can lead efforts toward increasing the number of seductive teachers presently employed in schools, not to mention new ones coming in.

Why English teachers? Well, they are scholars and students of language, a major instrument for learning and a powerful tool for *negotiating* and *persuading*, two key processes for effecting sensible school reform. Seductive English teachers are potentially invaluable resources for policymakers, administrators, and others who are interested in helping all students and teachers do better work. English teachers can negotiate with their colleagues and others an understanding that language is everybody's business in school, that natural connections exist between language and learning. They can demonstrate the power of these connections in their own teaching and in their relationships with colleagues. Any school reform movement, to be lasting and right, must have seductive teachers at its center to do this negotiating and persuading, and English teachers are best prepared and equipped to do that job. They must become the catalysts for educational reform by seizing and accepting opportunities for leadership—leadership of students, colleagues, administrators, and policymakers.

What are the key problems that schools face as we enter the twenty-first century? What must teachers—especially English teachers—know and believe that can help solve these problems? How do such teachers work? As we ask and answer questions like these, we trust that you will do your part as a reader and ultimately as an activist in helping schools attract, support, and keep good teachers. Maybe you're one yourself—or about to be.

References

Adams, Henry. 1931. *The Education of Henry Adams*. New York: The Modern Library.

Cushing, Harvey. 1925. *The Life of William Osler*, volume II. Oxford: The Clarendon Press.

De Witt, Karen. 1994. "The Huffingtons of Washington believe that social revolution begins at home." *The New York Times*, 22 May.

Glasser, William. 1990. *The Quality School*. New York, NY: Harper Perennial.

Haberman, Martin. 1994. "The Top Ten Fantasies of School Reformers." *Phi Delta Kappan* 75 (9): 689–672.

Hardy, Thomas. 1972. *Tess of the D'Urbervilles*, ed. Jean McMullan. New York: Amsco School Publications.

Hinsdale, Burke H. 1882. *President Garfield and Education*: Hiram College Memorial. Boston: James R. Osgood.

Salinger, J.D. 1945. *The Catcher in the Rye*. New York, NY: Bantam Books.

"Say Again." 1996. *The Virginian-Pilot*, 14 April.

Stevenson, Robert Louis. 1894. "The Suicide Club," in *New Arabian Nights*. New York, NY: Books, Inc., Publishers.

The Random House Dictionary of the English Language. 1987. New York, NY: Random House.

Vonnegut, Kurt. 1981. "How to Write with Style." In *Palm Sunday*. New York, NY: Prentice-Hall.

von Goethe, Johann Wolfgang. 1963. *Elective Affinities*, trans. Elizabeth Mayer and Louise Bogan. Chicago, IL: Henry Regnery Co.

Wallis, Claudia. 1994. "A Class of Their Own." *Time* 144 (18): 53–61.

Chapter Two

Moving Deck Chairs Around on the *Titanic*

We were on an airplane recently when a flight attendant, preparing for takeoff, addressed the passengers, "In case you haven't been in an automobile for the past twenty-five years, let me explain to you how to fasten your seat belts." As we write this, we feel a little like him. The conditions under which teachers work in schools today seem patently obvious; yet, we feel obliged to address some of those conditions now.

The media declare that schools are in deep trouble, and it's getting deeper. Over a decade ago the U.S. Department of Education released a now-familiar report, *A Nation at Risk*, proclaiming the failure of pubic education. A "rising tide of mediocrity," it said, is washing over the country's schools (1983, 5). For a government document on education, the report received unprecedented public attention. It launched more than a decade-long attack on American schools. In fact, panic set in. One "reform movement" after another sprang up, promising to "fix" things. But many of these movements pursued policies, principles, and practices that are very much like "moving deck chairs around on the *Titanic*." David Berliner and Bruce Biddle, two prominent psychologists interested in education, assess many of the current reform movements this way, "Damaging programs for educational reform have been adopted, a great deal of money has been wasted, effective school programs have been harmed, and morale has declined among educators" (1995, 4). We are willing to concede that the motivating forces behind these reform movements have been generally well-meaning, but Berliner and Biddle are not so sure. They argue quite persuasively that the movements have often been spurred by political ". . . desires to scapegoat educators as a way of diverting attention from America's deepening social problems . . ." (7). Whatever the case, many school improvement initiatives have tended to reflect a disturbing recklessness, desperation, and misplaced focus.

Many reformers have recommended warmed-over versions of "changes" that have been advocated and tried before, to little or no positive effect on actual student achievement or classroom practice. Linda Darling-Hammond, professor of education and codirector of the National Center for Restructuring Education, Schools, and Teaching at Columbia University, suggests that any approach to reform that focuses on ". . . tightening the controls: more courses, more tests, more directive curricula, more standards enforced by more rewards and more sanctions . . . " is an old approach that has not worked. She further observes, "Top-down directives are based on the presumption that teachers cannot be trusted to make sound decisions about curriculum and teaching" (1993, 755).

But permit us to pause for a moment here, to invite you to take a deep breath, relax, and dream a little. Try to think back to "simpler" times. As a former student, how do *you* remember school? Your answer is quite likely to influence your own views about how to "fix" schools today. For many of us, memories of school are filtered through a haze of inexact and romantic snippets of time, especially if we are looking back over decades. School, as we might imagine it, was a place where we went to be with friends and learn our lessons from teachers who "covered the curriculum." Students who were disruptive were "dealt with" quickly and misconduct was not allowed. If it occurred, it was punished. Teachers were somehow different from other adults we knew. They were authority figures who told us "truths," demanded that we do our best, cared for our minds and nurtured our spirits, and gave us tests to see how well or poorly we had learned what school offered us. We never thought of teachers and administrators as regular people, and if we ever saw them in routine places like grocery stores, service stations, restaurants, or theaters, we were genuinely surprised. We couldn't imagine their lives outside of school. Our school days constituted a bittersweet time of pain and pleasure. Our academic work was rigorous, we might recall, but we managed to get through it. In fact, the academic part of school may have been the least of our worries. Our major concerns had to do with extra-class activities—dances, dates, parties, movies, school clubs, school plays, athletic events, assemblies, hall talk, band trips, our first driver's license, and (finally) graduation.

There's likely to be something in this list for everyone, something to trigger both good and bad memories. In some extremely romanticized cases, we might even remember our own schools as existing in places—like Garrison Keillor's Lake Wobegon—"where all the women are strong, all the men are good lookin', and all the children are above average."

From indulging in this culturally simple and singular memory trip, or one that resembles it, we are liable to come away not only with a vision of how school was but how also it should be. But that vision can get us into trouble because school was never quite like our memories of it. We cannot go back to something that never really was. Even if our memories could be explicit and exact, we cannot re-create for the future what might have gone before. Those culturally simple and singular schools we might remember were the "old order"; the "new order" of schools at the end of the twentieth century is culturally complex and plural in every conceivable sense. In its details, it is also unprecedented in American education.

The new order of schools, like everything else, is difficult and dangerous to generalize about, but it is important to catch some glimpse of it if we are to acquire even a basic vision of what teachers today are dealing with in classrooms. A useful way to begin developing this modern sense of school is to regard our society as a whole, if that's possible. The snapshot we attempt to offer here is intended as a reminder, not as astoundingly new information. (If you've been paying even casual attention to the media lately, you can predict much of what we will say now.)

We'll start with an indisputable fact: America is an increasingly dangerous place to live. Crime rates in every major city are alarmingly high, and going up in suburbs and small towns, as well. People carry guns and use them to settle disputes or to get their own way. Since Watergate brought down a President over twenty years ago, citizens have stopped trusting anyone who would seize the mantle of leadership in government at any level. Greed dominates the economic landscape in more obvious and publicized ways than ever before. Most citizens saw the 1994 major league baseball strike as a greedy dispute among multimillionaire owners and players, whose *minimum* salary more than triples American teachers' *highest*. Children of middle-and-above income families, we are told, will never "have it so good" as their parents. Our natural environment has been depleted and damaged beyond repair. Many Americans' perceptions at the end of the twentieth century are that our national conscience and value system have collapsed, our leaders and heroes (arguably few, if any, left) have clay feet; our future is bleak;

and we seem to have little knowledge or resolve to do anything about the situation. A cartoon we have before us shows a television newscaster reporting, "The world went to hell in a handbasket today, and the State Department is studying the situation." We are a nation of skeptics, cynics, and narcissists in unprecedented numbers. Clearly, there is good reason we have become so. Of course, things have been bad before, very bad. They seem, however, to be getting worse, and despite what some might like, we cannot go back to supposedly simpler, slower times.

So how does this affect our nation's youth? Badly, of course. Many young people—especially (but in no way exclusively) those in desperate economic and social circumstances—have low expectations for their future. Judging from the general decline and decay of nearly everything and everyone around them, they see a dim and dismal road ahead. Our teenage suicide rate is shocking; drug abuse and violence are out of control; pernicious cults and gangs abound; many students (and teachers) are scared to go to school and even more scared after they get there; media reports of national test scores say that students today achieve less than both their predecessors and their counterparts in other lands; and—following Generation X—young people understandably wonder who they are and what they're doing here. Granted, the youthful "identity crisis" is a common phenomenon—every generation endures it. But this one seems deeper, more poignant, and more ominous than that endured by youth before. Thoughtful people might argue (and often do) that the world has always been a tough place to grow up in. In this century alone, we've seen at least one (some would say more) devastating economic depression, two World Wars and several tragic "conflicts," the threat of nuclear annihilation, and other crises of frightening proportions. Up to now, however, humanity has always prevailed. Problems get resolved or, at least, ameliorated, and the world feels better for a while. What is different in the minds of many young people today, though, is a sense that *this time* we've hit the wall. We've seriously screwed up. We've run the course, the end is in sight, and it doesn't look good. Furthermore, we're to blame. We've done it to ourselves. The Soviet Empire didn't "bury us" as it threatened to do in the 60s, but we are burying ourselves. There will not be much for youth to inherit. We have fulfilled the prophecy of Pogo, "We have met the enemy, and it is us."

On that happy note, how does what we are observing and opining here affect the nation's schools? As we said in Chapter One, every school is but a reflection of the complex cultural character that defines the community it serves. To extend that proposition, we might also offer that schools in general reflect the complex cultural character of society as a whole. These statements are but echoes of what many others have noted before about the symbiotic relationship between school and society. If the echoes are accurate, teachers are dealing with understandably troubled, scared, confused, and grim youth, who mirror all the characteristics and afflictions that define America in the last decade of the twentieth century.

Some observers claim that things like drug dealing, illiteracy, robbery, and murder have replaced gum chewing, turning in papers late, tardiness, and talking in class as the new problems for today's schools. Given the several issues we could choose to elaborate on now, we choose only two. We believe these two occupy the minds of teachers every morning they enter their classrooms. They are problems endemic to far too many schools, and they are ugly. We are speaking of the *violence* problem and the *literacy* problem. We wish to examine these problems and to suggest how good teachers attempt to deal with them.

First, the violence problem. How bad is it? Some of the statistics are sobering. *NEA Today*, a publication of the National Education Association, reports that the number of children killed by firearms between 1979 and 1991 equals the number of Americans killed in the Vietnam War; that every two hours, a child dies from gunshots; that guns kill more black males between the ages of ten and twenty-four than any other cause (Merina 1994, 27). A 1993 Harris survey, reported in *Youth Record*, says that twenty-two percent of students polled claimed they took weapons to school in the previous school year (10). A Gallup poll conducted for *Phi Delta Kappan* in 1993 showed the public ranking drug abuse, discipline, and violence in the top four of the ten most serious problems affecting schools (Elam, 137–152). The depressing facts and numbers drone on. We will not belabor what has become all too common.

Yet a MetLife teachers' survey in 1993 showed that seventy-seven percent of teachers and fifty percent of students felt safe in and around their own schools (9). According to a *New York Times* article on August 13, 1994, although violent incidents in New York City's 1,100 public schools (K–12) rose twenty-six percent in 1993–1994, no homicides occurred in them. Still, in the same article, former New York City Schools' Chancellor Ramon C. Cortines lamented, "When I read the list of weapons we have seized, I wonder if we shouldn't start handing out medals for valor instead of report cards" (27). Clearly, the new order of schools in America is far more threatening and dangerous to the physical lives of teachers and youth than the old order was. The violence factor defines a major difference between schools today and the schools adults remember, looking back over decades. But we cannot go home again.

One significant aspect of the violence problem has to do with the social dynamics of inner cities. Many young residents there are victims of a street culture characterized by daily violence, springing from the desperate circumstances of poverty, which breeds hopelessness. Writing particularly about the plight of young African American men, Elijah Anderson, eminent sociologist at the University of Pennsylvania, describes "the code of the streets," at the heart of which is the issue of *respect.* Anderson notes,

> The person whose very appearance—including his clothing, demeanor, and way of moving—deters transgressions feels that he possesses and may be considered by others to possess, a measure of respect. With the right amount of respect . . . he can avoid "being bothered" in public. If he is bothered, not only may he be in physical danger but he has been disgraced or "dissed" (disrespected). Many of the forms that dissing can take might seem petty to middle-class people (maintaining eye contact for too long, for example), but to those invested in the street code, these actions become serious indications of the other person's intentions (1994, 82).

Of course, such attitudes and behaviors exist in schools as well as in the streets. Anderson claims that the code of the streets is rooted in a "lack of faith in the police and the judicial system," but he might have included the schools, as well. He writes, ". . . the street code emerges where the influence of the police ends and personal responsibility for one's safety is felt to begin" (83). When youngsters perceive school as an unsafe place, the code of the street prevails. Anderson says, ". . . the street-oriented home may be fraught with anger, verbal disputes, physical aggression, and even mayhem. The children observe these goings-on, learning the lesson that might makes right" (83). As seductive teachers know (in or out of school), no teaching technique rivals modeling in effectiveness. When students see the same modeling going on in school, even to a lesser degree, that they see in their homes (angry and abusive outbursts from teachers, for example), the behaviors they learned early in life get validated, and they respond in kind. Seductive teachers know, at least, that if there is any hope for leading and attracting students toward more civil behaviors, and winning students over to those behaviors, then teachers themselves must provide more civil models than those that students encounter in their homes and on the streets. Schools must provide significantly alternative models for such youngsters; schools must create genuinely attractive, alternative, learning communities. In short, schools have to defeat the streets in the seduction game. To do so, teachers must *decide to lead.*

What further compounds the problem is something we might call "the baddest dude" phenomenon. That is, there is a role played out by some street-oriented youngsters, at school and elsewhere, that is especially grim. It's a role played by the student who all teachers, even seductive ones, dread to see enter their classrooms. This is the "hard-core" student, often male, who wears his "manhood" on his sleeve. His main goal, it seems, is to show everyone around him that he has no fear, that he doesn't care about anyone or anything, that he has "nerve." As Anderson writes, "Nerve is shown when one takes another person's possessions (the more valuable the better), 'messes with' someone's woman, throws the first punch, 'gets in someone's face,' or pulls a trigger" (92). This is the student who doesn't just respond to violence; he (or she) starts it. Such students have deeply internalized the code of the streets. They have learned their lessons well. In fact, they have gone beyond the street "curriculum." Can school reach such students? Some would say not—even *absolutely* not. Some would suggest—have suggested—sticking them in boot camps, holding tanks, or prison. Radical, last-ditch solutions, indeed. We, however (in our most romantic moments), think the answer is yes, or at least maybe. Such students can change their lives, with help. There are teachers who are touching those lives, helping to transform them, as we write this, perhaps as you are reading.

Seductive teachers tend to understand deeply the cultures of their schools and communities. They have both intuitive and learned knowledge about how their students might behave in a variety of circumstances. They work hard from day one of any school year to build safe learning environments that belong mutually to all who enter them. They are able to lead, attract, and win over students in believing in the efficacy of a civilized life. We wish now to endorse a strategy that is being tried in many schools today, one that can go a long way toward alleviating, if not solving altogether, the violence problem. It is a strategy that good teachers employ, with many variations, anyway, but we believe it should become integrated formally into the school curriculum—particularly, but in no way exclusively, in urban settings. The strategy we are speaking of is mediation.

The sole business of school is schooling, schooling that enables students to become independent, problem-solving, decision-making, thoughtful people who value themselves, others, and the society in which they live. This view of public schooling is solidly grounded in our national need to prepare citizens for democracy, as our Founding Fathers saw it. If this vision still holds (and some deem that proposition questionable), the solution to any school problem should have an educational value within the context of the school's purpose as we have sketched it.

While they are necessary in extreme cases, strategies of surveillance and close administrative supervision of students in schools are not a sufficient answer to the violence problem. In the long run they, too, are like "moving deck chairs around on the *Titanic*." Such currently common strategies as installing metal detectors, creating "hot lines" for students and teachers to report trouble, placing guards in hallways, and enacting more federal and state laws may be helpful as tools for "crisis management." We would not argue against such strategies in some cases. To do so would be naive and reckless, given the scary dimensions of the violence problem in many schools today. But ultimately what schools need are people and programs to educate students better about how to resolve conflicts and disputes. To state the matter as boldly as we can, students must be surrounded by psychologically and emotionally powerful adults, adults with healthy habits of mind and behavior.

Such organizations as the National Institute for Citizen Education in the Law and the National Crime Prevention Council are on the right track. They are working to promote the process of mediation as a long-term strategy for dealing with the violence problem in schools. Mediation has long been used by the legal profession as an alternative to taking cases to court, where judges or juries settle disputes. Of course, there are times when going to court is necessary, like going to a school principal's office. Mediation, however, is a process of managing conflicts through an objective third party (mediator) whose job is to get adversaries to solve their own disputes with a goal of eliminating further trouble in the future. Typically there are six steps in the mediating process (Zimmer 1993, 19):

1. Introduction. The mediator makes the parties *feel at ease* and explains the ground rules. The mediator's role is not to make a decision but to help the parties reach a mutually acceptable agreement. The mediator explains that he/she will not take sides. Confidentiality is explained to the parties.

2. Telling the Story. Each party *tells what happened*. The person bringing the complaint usually tells his/her side first, without interruption. Then the other party tells his/her story.

3. Identifying Facts/Issues. The mediator attempts to identify agreed-upon facts and to identify the needs of the disputants. This is done by *actively listening* to each side, summarizing

each party's view, and asking if these are the facts as each party understands them. Sometimes the mediator will ask the disputants to summarize each other's perspective.

4. Identifying Alternative Solutions. The disputants think of *possible solutions* to the problem. The mediator makes a list and then asks each party to explain his/her feelings about each possibility.

5. Revising and Discussing Solutions. Based on the feelings of the parties involved, the mediator revises possible solutions and attempts to identify *common ground*.

6. Reaching an Agreement. The mediator helps parties reach an agreement, which is written. The parties discuss what will happen if either fails to follow it.

Seductive teachers, by their training, intuition, and/or experience, have generally internalized this fundamental process. They tend to follow its principles in encounters with students. They know that one of their main functions as effective teachers is to make all students "feel at ease" in their classrooms (step one). They know the importance of allowing students to "tell their stories," whether those stories have to do with academic learning or settling disputes (step two). They fully understand the necessity, the power, and the value of "active listening" (step three); they do it themselves, and they work to help students learn to do it. They recognize that a critical aspect of learning anything is to consider "alternative solutions" to problems (step four). They recognize that one of the important roles they play in classrooms is to build a sense of belonging, of community, among all who gather there, thereby helping students find common ground with one another as learners and as school citizens (step five). And they help students find and register points of agreement (step six), while respecting cultural diversity and intellectual divergence, both of which are often present in rich learning environments. Seductive teachers tend to run their classrooms according to such principles as these, principles that define much of what all seductive teachers share in common as they relate to students and colleagues.

Schools of the 90s and beyond, however, require that these principles be shared. Seductive teachers must take the lead in helping their colleagues learn them, or rediscover them; and, of course, students must learn them. Across the subject areas and grade range of schools, students must be taught how to mediate and solve their own problems and disputes. Anything less is mere crisis management— necessary perhaps, in the short term—but certainly not sufficient if the violence problem is to be solved for the long term. Teachers must take the initiative to promote, to practice, and to teach the principles of conflict management to whoever needs to learn them. No mandate or quick-fix from the outside can be nearly so successful as thoughtful diligence by seductive teachers, meeting regularly with students and colleagues and working collaboratively on a daily basis.

Leading, attracting, and winning over—our definition of seductive teaching—are the crucial goals for teachers interested in contributing to genuine school reform. Principles of mediation—feeling at ease, telling one's story, listening actively, examining alternatives, finding common ground—are not only sound principles of mediation, they are also sound principles for teaching. They are equally sound principles for teachers as school reformers to follow as they lead their colleagues. These principles work not only in classrooms with students but also in faculty meetings, inservice workshops, and other settings where efforts are made to help *all* teachers do better work.

We turn now to a second problem on the minds of teachers every morning they enter their classrooms: the literacy problem. It is connected to the violence problem. As former First Lady Barbara Bush once declared, quoted by Stanley Wellborn in a *U.S. News and World Report* article,

> Most people don't know we spend 6.6 billion dollars a year to keep 750,000 illiterates in jail. I'm trying to remind people that there's a direct correlation between crime and illiteracy, between illiteracy and unemployment. (1982, 53)

Yet, the U.S. Bureau of the Census reported in 1979 that 99.5 percent of American adults could read and write (85)! The methodology that led to this report, however—written questionnaires and telephone interviews—has been challenged, even ridiculed. Six years after the report appeared, Johnathan Kozol produced a startling book, *Illiterate America*, in which he cites such statistics as these: Sixty million people, or more than a third of our nation's adult population, either cannot read or read at a level that Kozol describes as "less than equal to the full survival needs of our society"; fifteen percent of recent graduates from urban high schools read below a sixth grade level; eighty-five percent of juveniles who come to court as alleged criminals are functionally illiterate; of 158 nations in the United Nations, the United States ranks forty-ninth in literacy levels (1985, 10). Kozol further claims that many daily newspapers in America are written at about a tenth-grade level, and magazines such as *Time* and *Newsweek* at about a twelfth-grade level (16). If he is even close to being right, a shockingly high percentage of American adults do not have access to reading materials, which literate adults read routinely and take for granted. All this represents America over a decade ago.

The situation may have improved some but not appreciably. Citing a U.S. Department of Education report, Carl Sagan and Ann Druyan reported in a 1994 issue of *Parade Magazine* that over forty million American adults are illiterate or barely literate (5). (They acknowledge that other estimates are higher.) The media continue to flood us with reports from the National Assessment of Educational Progress and the Educational Testing Service, claiming that American students' school achievement lags behind that of their counterparts in other countries like Germany and Japan. The literacy problem seems to surround us; like the violence problem, it's like a sore that won't heal. But we believe in taking a longer view.

Remember when the word *literacy* meant the ability to read and write? Today it is commonly used as a tag word in phrases like *computer literacy, cultural literacy, mathematical literacy, scientific literacy*, and even *personal literacy*. We believe it is time to launch a rescue mission for the word *literacy*. For our purposes here, we wish *literacy* to mean the ability to read and write. We're not going "back to basics" on this point, however, at least in the conventional sense. We do not mean *literacy* the way the U.S. Bureau of the Census meant it in 1979—"the ability to read and write a simple message." We mean it the way we think seductive teachers mean it—the ability to engage actively in the cultural conversations necessary for rewarding work, play, personal growth, citizenship, and human relationships. This is reading and writing made large, reading and writing as processes of critical and creative thinking. We do not hear, read, write, or speak *just* language in its usual sense but also tone, style, intent, and occasion.

For example, by *read*, we mean the ability to make meaning from many kinds of texts (print, film, nonverbal language) and contexts (space, temporal events, human interaction). That is to say, school must help the young learn how to read a book, read a film (most certainly to include commercial advertising), and read a gesture or any other kind of nonverbal expression. It must also help the young read all sorts of situational events. School must help the young develop habits of inquiry, of asking "What (and how) does this mean?" about everything. How much power is there, for example, in being able to read the following?

- a sincere/insincere motivation
- a real/false friendship
- a helping/hurting hand

- a healthy/unhealthy invitation
- an honest/deceitful behavior
- a safe/unsafe occasion
- a genuine/sarcastic comment
- an authentic/illusory event
- a winning/losing attitude
- a smart/dumb decision
- a good/rotten deal

Answer? A lot. Reading means interpreting and evaluating—*making sense*—not merely recognizing details and recalling them on cue.

Further, by *write*, we mean composing meaning through language, and many instruments exist for composing—words, certainly, but also paint, music, clay, and the human body (through drama and dance). These views of reading and writing are expansive but nonetheless necessary to living rich lives and coping with events, ideas, issues, and other people. Our definition of literacy goes way beyond the mere ability "to read and write a simple message." The literacy we are advocating is to be taken in its historical/literal sense (reading and writing as comprehending and producing language, of course) but also in its current/metaphoric/culturally plural sense (reading and writing as inventing and reinventing many worlds, both inner and outer).

In addition, we wish to attempt something of a rescue mission for teachers here, as well. In light of such sobering and depressing statistics as we have reported on the violence and literacy problems, any responsible citizen is understandably concerned about the teaching profession's ability to teach literacy. With such a focus on all that is amiss in our society and, therefore, our schools, it is no wonder that Americans are concerned. Even worse, many of our citizens have become afflicted with an unaccustomed feeling of inferiority to the rest of the developed nations of the world. So let us remind you of the statistician who drowned trying to cross a river with an average depth of three feet. Teachers and students are doing better work than many people know. To cite Berliner and Biddle again, from *The Manufactured Crisis*, on the Scholastic Aptitude Test,". . . since 1976 . . . scores increased for every minority group during this period" (1995, 20). Further, "When school achievements are steady or even improve in a society that is falling apart, we think that educators have pulled off a miracle. It is time to celebrate the public schools of the nation, not to blame them" (29).

So let's pause to celebrate excellent teachers and engaged students everywhere. Consider this classroom scenario as emblematic of what might go on in an English class taught by a master teacher. Ms. S. is about to teach a short poem, "Poem 39," by Charles Reznikoff. She is committed to an inquiry-oriented, student-centered approach. The class session might go as follows:

Ms. S.: What do you own that you think you couldn't live without? Something electrical or mechanical. For me, it's my watch. I couldn't do without it. What's like that for you? Yes, Fred.

Fred: Telephone.

Ms. S.: Why?

Fred: Gotta call people. Gotta be called.

Ms. S.: Rhonda?

Rhonda: Blow dryer. I couldn't go out of the house if I didn't have a blow dryer!

Ms. S.: No bad hair days for you, right Rhonda? O.K. Sam?

Sam: Lights, man.

Ms. S.: Electric lights, yeah. That's really getting down to basics. It would be hard to get by without lights. What else? Krista?

Krista: TV. I gotta have TV.

Ms. S.: Why's that important to you?

Krista: Well, that's how you get news, find out about the weather, MTV, *you* know.

Ms. S.: Right. Danny?

Danny: Computer.

Ms. S.: Why?

Danny: Play games. Surf the 'net. Stuff like that.

Ms. S.: O.K. Watches, telephones, hair dryers, TVs, computers—these things are important. Let me ask you, by having such things, are we giving up anything? What did people do before we had them? Lights, for example.

Kevin: People used candles, I guess.

Beth: Yeah, and they probably went to bed earlier and got up earlier, too.

Ms. S.: So these things have changed our lives, have they? O.K. Let's look at this poem and see if it says anything like what we've been talking about.

(Ms. S. turns on the overhead and students see "In Our Street." Ms. S. asks Tanya to read these lines aloud.)

> What are you doing in our street among the automobiles, horse?
>
> How are your cousins, the centaur, and the unicorn?

Ms. S.: Why do you think the poet is asking these questions?

(No responses)

Ms. S.: Is there anything electrical or mechanical in this poem?

Kathy: The automobile.

Ms. S.: Is the car in this poem like the things we talked about earlier—like watches and telephones and TV?

Robin: Well, yeah, that's something that would be hard to do without.

Ms. S.: Has the car made our lives easier?

Robin: Yeah, but harder, too.

Ms. S.: Why?

Robin: Because it's caused pollution and a lot of people get killed in car accidents.

Deborah: Maybe things were better when we had horses.

Ms. S.: How? Have we given up clean air to have cars?

Deborah: Well, I mean, like Robin said, if we still got around on horses, we'd have cleaner air and a lot of people would still be alive.

Ms. S.: So, when we get something, we give up something?

Ken: There you go. The car's a good thing, but it causes problems.

Ms. S.: What advantages do you think we had in the day of the horse and buggy that we don't have now?

Fred: Life was a lot slower then.

Ms. S.: How?

Fred: It took longer to get places on a horse.

Krista: Maybe people stayed home more, too.

Deborah: So the car made life faster, which is good, but the horse slowed people down, which is also good.

Ms. S.: Have any of you ever felt out of place anywhere?

Fred: Yeah.

Ms. S.: When, Fred?

Fred: Right now. Am I the only one who doesn't know what a centaur and a unicorn are?

Ms. S.: Does anyone know?

(No responses. Ms. S. changes transparencies on the overhead to show pictures of a centaur and a unicorn.)

Ms. S.: O.K. We've got six dictionaries in the back of the room, so get into groups of four and use the dictionaries to figure out which one of these is which.

(Five minutes later, the groups have their answers.)

Ms. S.: So why do you think the poet is asking these questions?

John: It seems like he's saying a lot of what we've been saying. The horse and the centaur and the unicorn are out of place with the automobile.

Ms. S.: So?

Fred: Yeah, and the automobile might even go away, too, like everything else. Nothing lasts forever.

Ms. S.: So?

Fred: So we should appreciate what we have? Is that what he's saying in the poem?

Ms. S.: O.K. Now, while you're in your groups, see if anyone knows what the words *rhetorical question* mean. If no one does, look it up in the dictionary. See if what you find out has anything to do with this poem. Then, talk in your groups about why you think the poet calls the unicorn and centaur the horse's "cousins." Also, remember when we read *The Catcher in the Rye* and *Inherit the Wind?* Look at these two transparencies and talk about what Holden and Drummond might have meant in these lines, in light of what we've been saying about the Reznikoff poem.

(Ms. S. uses two overhead projectors to show the following lines from Holden Caulfield (*Catcher*) and defense attorney Drummond (*Inherit the Wind*), respectively):

> I don't even like old cars. I mean they don't even interest me. I'd rather have a . . . horse. A horse is at least human . . . .(1962, 131)

> Gentlemen, progress has never been a bargain. You've got to pay for it. Sometimes I think there's a man behind a counter who says, "All right, you can have a telephone; but you'll have to give up privacy, the charm of distance. Madam, you may vote, but at a price; you lose the right to retreat behind a powder-puff or a petticoat. Mister, you may conquer the air; but the birds will lose their wonder, and the clouds will smell of gasoline. (Lawrence and Lee 1995, 53–53)

In this classroom discussion, the teacher uses inquiry as a method of seduction. She teases out experiential responses that enable students to think as they need to when they encounter the Reznikoff poem—this strategy is an example of what "reading readiness" is about for her. She treats her students as a community of thinking learners who are discovering literature as a pathway into deep thought and the exploration of values. (John says, "The horse and the centaur and the unicorn are out of place with the automobile." Fred says, "Nothing lasts forever. . . . So we should appreciate what we have?") These students are not reading Reznikoff's poem for information, for what Louise Rosenblatt, influential literary theorist, calls *efferent* reading (1978, 24); they are reading it to make meaning and to discover the suggestive power of poetic expression. In this sense—using Rosenblatt's term again—students are having an *aesthetic* experience with literature (25). And the literacy they are achieving is a literacy defined as engagement in the cultural conversations necessary for rewarding work, play, personal growth, citizenship, and human relationships.

Tomorrow, when students discuss rhetorical questions and other matters, they may begin to think of the writing of poems as the art of license. Their conversation may lead to discussing the differences between poetry and prose, in which case Ms. S. might at some point quote Coleridge, as cited by Joseph Green, "Prose, words in their best order; poetry, the *best* words in their best order" (1995, 1529). She might write on the board the name of poet Alberto Blanco and its translation, Al White, then get students talking about which name seems more poetic (if either does). They may engage in resistant talk, like "Why do we have to read so much poetry? People in the world don't read poetry." In which case Ms. S. might eventually point out that poetry clubs are springing up all across the country, rivaling comedy clubs, or that more than 400 poetry magazines appear on the Internet, or that around 1,000 volumes of poetry are published per year.

Further, through the references to Holden Caulfield and defense attorney Drummond, Ms. S. may lead students to recognize the value of reading *across* literature as well as *into* it—the value, that is, of intertextual reading. Ms. S. and her students may creep up on the notion that, like progress, people's words and deeds have consequences, too, thus bringing issues of both violence and literacy into focus simultaneously. Tomorrow someone might inquire, "Why would anyone today be *interested* in poetry?" And Ms. S. eventually may offer that when things get confused and jumbled politically and sociologically, people often hunger for another language, a language that touches them. That may lead to new directions of thought and talk in the classroom. She may lead students to consider that *feeling is first*, that people are hungry to *feel*. Who knows what other territories Ms. S. and her students might touch as they journey together through this unit on "Gain and Loss"?

As we've said, there are many teachers doing good work. Even statistical evidence supports this assumption, as Berliner and Biddle have shown. Further, in a 1994 issue of *Education Week*, educational researcher Gerald Bracey reports that eighty-six percent of American students are currently graduating from high school, and sixty percent of them go on to college—this in a relatively young nation now trying admirably to educate all of its citizens (33). Such has not always been the case in America. In 1800, for example, women and minorities had no voice in government, and only white, male, property owners could vote. In an important sense, we can be justifiably proud of huge strides taken in the progress of American education during the last one-hundred years, particularly. We must remind ourselves that the critical problem of literacy in America is a phenomenon of the twentieth century, maybe of just the last four decades—i.e., literacy as we are defining it: the ability to read and write at levels that enable people to engage actively in the cultural conversations necessary for rewarding work, play, personal growth, citizenship, and human relationships now and in the future. Given this definition of literacy, teachers' jobs are admittedly harder than they used to be in the old order of school days. But seductive teachers have always done their jobs well, as they continue to do. At the moment, however, we simply do not have enough of them in our schools. Our prescription for reform is to use all available resources to put more of them there, and clear the paths for them to help their colleagues become seductive teachers, as well.

In *The Quality School*, William Glasser defines an effective teacher this way, ". . . one who is able to convince not half or three quarters but essentially all of his or her students to do quality work in school" (1990, 14). A high standard, indeed. Glasser goes on to say that teachers must be *leaders*, not *bosses*. We couldn't agree more. As we have said, seductive teachers lead, and they are able to attract students to seeing school as a safe and stimulating place that can nurture their growth; ultimately, seductive teachers win students over to accepting the opportunities for learning that school provides. Of course, seductive teachers know that only the learner can do the learning (a concept Mr. Ditto never really grasped). They know that at the heart of their jobs lies "heart" itself—i.e., the unflagging determination to believe in all learners (and in all teachers), even when students and colleagues do not appear to believe in themselves. Herein lies the challenge, and seductive teachers not only accept it but respond to it often with amazing rates of success, especially when they decide to lead.

When it comes to reading and writing, then, how do teachers go about leading, attracting, and winning over students and colleagues to doing better work? Does the answer lie in effective uses of textbooks, workbooks, "skill drills," lectures, tests, and technology? Does it lie in teachers' scholarly knowledge of what they are teaching? Not really, as important as such things certainly are. A more direct and fundamental answer lies in developing in students certain attitudes and dispositions for learning that cause students to honor and respect it, and *to value themselves and others*. Of course, the details of this answer are complex. If the answer were simple, it would hardly be worth this space, our energy, and your time. For some of those details, we find Sheridan Blau's dimensions of what he calls "personal literacy" instructive. (Blau is a National Writing Project site director and English professor at the University of California, Santa Barbara.) The following, cited in a chapter by Carole Bencich, appears in *Global Voices: Culture and Identity in the Teaching of English*:

1. capacity for sustained focused attention
2. willingness to suspend closure—to entertain problems rather than avoid them
3. willingness to take risks—to predict and be wrong, to respond honestly
4. tolerance for failure: willingness to reread and reread again
5. tolerance for ambiguity, paradox, and uncertainty
6. . . . willingness to change mind, to appreciate alternative visions, and to engage in . . . believing as well as doubting (1994, 174)

While Blau refers to these as dimensions of personal literacy, we prefer to think of them as "dispositions for learning." Seductive teachers know these dispositions well, and they value them in classrooms. They are strikingly similar to learning principles inherent within the mediation process that we advocated earlier in connection with the violence problem. They are similar because, as Gertrude Stein might have put it, good learning principles are good learning principles are good learning principles....

Seductive teachers model what Blau refers to as a "capacity for focused attention." When they themselves read in their classrooms—as they often do, both silently and aloud—they read actively, i.e., they focus completely on a text and their personal responses to it. They lead students toward an understanding and a habit of reading in this way. They attract students to texts by helping them see the relationships of textual (and intertextual) content to their own lives. Eventually, they win students over to the art and appreciation of reading for personal meaning, not merely for remembering factual details that may appear on tests. Seductive teachers know, and they help students realize, that focused attention is critical to learning. They are able to "sell" that view to students, and sometimes it's a hard sell. They also lead students toward discovering it for themselves. This principle is like the Buddhist adage, "When you run, run; when you walk, walk. Don't wobble." In other words, seductive teachers remind students in their classrooms, as often as necessary, "When we play, we will play; when we read and write, we will read and write; we will focus on what we are doing when we are doing it." Through the practice of this learning principle—and seductive teachers' abilities to help students understand, practice, and value it—students learn major lessons in self-discipline and in learning how to learn.

Seductive teachers insist that students *suspend closure* as they read texts and write their own. As a result, students come to see problems as learning adventures as opposed to discouraging obstacles. Seductive teachers lead students toward developing a sense of school as a place to encounter, define, and solve problems, and that makes school engaging, not boring. In seductive teachers' classrooms, young people behave as real readers and writers, not merely as students of a reading and writing class. They learn to *expect* problems and questions to emerge and to view them as opportunities. To use a cliché, they begin to see their glasses as half-full rather than half-empty when difficult issues arise—e.g., issues in texts they are reading and texts they are writing.

In seductive teachers' classrooms, students develop a willingness to take riskS with their reading and writing. They know they will not be punished or ridiculed for making mistakes. Seductive teachers know and help students see that blundering and stumbling are parts of learning and growing. Such teachers are happy to show students that no two or more people see or do things in precisely the same ways, and good teachers value that divergence. Divergent thinking is encouraged and allowed as students respond and reconsider their reading and as they write and rewrite their own texts.

Seductive teachers help students acquire a *tolerance for failure* as readers and writers by letting them in on a closely guarded secret: that experts and professionals fail, too—often many times—before tasting the nectar of success. Many unsuccessful students are intimidated by the false perception that a "real" writer produces a polished draft on the first try, or that a "real" reader understands deeply the most intricate features of a text (print or otherwise) the first time through it. Seductive teachers lead students to a different, more accurate understanding—that what makes "real" readers and writers is perseverance and a dogged devotion to "getting it right" eventually. The seductive teacher may be heard saying things like the following: "If Herman Melville had *Moby Dick* back, you can bet he'd make some changes"; or, "on his deathbed, Johann Von Goethe, the great German philosopher, said he was still learning to read"; or, "Mark Twain once said that the difference between the exact word and the nearly exact word is the difference between lightning and the lightning bug." Seductive teachers press, cajole, tease, and otherwise challenge students—according to individual styles and personalities—to do it again, to take another look, to reflect some more, and to reevaluate their thinking as readers, writers, and learners.

Seductive teachers help students acquire a *tolerance for ambiguity, paradox, and uncertainty* in their reading and writing. Such teachers encourage students to look for more than one meaning, for apparent or real contradictions in what they read and write. Students learn that to be uncertain is not only permissible but necessary in the journey toward certainty. By listening to their classmates and others, by rethinking their own views and values, students often discover that truth is a twin, that answers often exist on both sides of a coin, not just one or the other. Seductive teachers, in short, encourage students to wait, and through the waiting comes a "truth," often ambiguous and paradoxical. But the waiting must always be active, not passive.

Students learn from seductive teachers a *willingness to change mind, to appreciate alternative visions.* After all, human beings used to believe the earth was flat, that smoking Chesterfield cigarettes was "good for you" (as Perry Como used to say on television in the early 60s), that women would never go to military schools, that a man would never walk on the moon (Did he? We know a high school teacher, Jim Yano in Virginia Beach, Virginia, who makes a powerful and persuasive case to his tenth-grade English students that a man did *not* walk on the moon, with the intention of getting students to hammer arguments back to him), that the Soviet Empire would never crumble, that the Berlin Wall would never fall, that Babe Ruth's single-season and career home run records would never be broken, that personal computers would never catch on, that human organs would never be transplantable, and so on. Seductive teachers work hard to release students from the notion that there is only one answer to everything, that "truth" is solid, concrete, and unchanging. In seductive teacher's classrooms, students read and write ardently but draw conclusions tentatively. In such classrooms, minds are always moving, changing. When that is the case, there is in progress a mighty war raging against illiteracy.

There is, then, to a large extent, an English curriculum solution to both the violence problem and the literacy problem. Whatever else "English" is, it's language—language that often invades the soul. Whatever the literature canon is that enobles that language, it must include works that deal with *conflict*—strenuous and wrenching conflict that likely will provoke many different ways of questioning, valuing, and perceiving. That doesn't mean literature by "dead white guys" only, or by any other group only, but it does mean literature deliberately chosen that can move the psyche up, down, and all around. A healthy learning tension occurs in classrooms where teachers and students openly and deeply interrogate texts, interrogate each other, and interrogate themselves. Through talking, reading, listening, writing, and viewing, with high degrees of both patience and rigor, students get better with language and more knowledgeable about alternative ways of dealing with conflicts; therefore, they are likely to get better and wiser at handling trouble when it arises in their own lives and relationships.

What if, for example, we were to place at the front of our classrooms this quotation from James Redfield's *The Celestine Prophecy?*

> . . . we humans have always sought to increase our personal
> energy in the only manner we have known: by seeking to
> psychologically steal it from others—an unconscious competi-
> tion that underlies all human conflict in the world. (1993, 65–66)

This passage suggests at least two questions we might ask students as they encounter literary characters in conflict. The questions might be framed in several ways, but here are two possibilities. What is the nature of "personal energy" that (so-and-so) is trying to "steal" from (so-and-so)? How does he or she try to "steal" it? Consider the questions in light of such pairs as Brutus and Caesar (from Shakespeare's *Julius Caesar*), "Pappy" and Huck (from Mark Twain's *The Adventures of Huckleberry Finn*), Jack and Ralph (from Golding's *Lord of the Flies*), Creon and Antigone (from Sophocles' *Antigone*), Ahab and the White Whale (from Melville's *Moby Dick*), the Socs and the Greasers (from S. E. Hinton's *The Outsiders*), Norton and John (from Paul Zindel's *The Pigman*), Doc Holliday and Johnny Ringo (from the films *Tombstone* and *Wyatt Earp*), Waverly Jong and her mother (from Amy Tan's *The Joy Luck Club*), and Mr. and Celie (from Alice Walker's *The Color Purple*).

Such considerations can deepen students' understanding of the psychology of human conflict, not only between fictional characters in literature but also between students themselves. Reflecting rationally upon the nature of human conflict can help students deal in healthier ways with challenges they face in their own lives. Such considerations can help us, as English teachers, realize major goals of the literature curriculum: to enrich students' lives and to aid personal growth, both of which are by-products of the development of literacy as we have defined and discussed it.

No one knows what particular piece of literature it might be— print or nonprint—that moves a young reader or viewer from point

A to point "somewhere else" in their lives, but you can make at least two safe bets. First, you can bet it will be literature that appeals to one or more of the basic needs that drive the human spirit. William Glasser calls these needs survival, love, power, freedom, and fun (43)—not a bad set of criteria for building a reading list, when you think about it, a literature curriculum perched upon branches of identified human needs. Also, you can bet it will often be controversial literature, offensive to somebody or several somebodies, because literature worth reading tends to arouse strong responses across a galaxy of world views. Probing these different world views defines a process for advancing both peace and literacy in schools and communities. Such probing—such perspective expansion—is critical to authentic school reform.

References

Anderson, Elijah. 1994. "The Code of the Streets." *Atlantic Monthly.* 81–94.

Becnich, Carole. 1994. "Humane Literacy: Literacy Competence and the Ways of Knowing." In *Global Voices: Cultural Identity and the Teaching of English*, ed. Joseph Milner and Carol Pope, 174–182. Urbana, IL: National Council of Teachers of English.

Berliner, David, and Biddle, Bruce. 1995. *The Manufactured Crisis.* Reading, MA: Addison-Wesley.

Bracey, Gerald. 1994. "What If Education Broke Out All Over." *Education Week*, 30 March.

Darling-Hammond, Linda. 1993. "Reforming the School Reform Agenda." *Phi Delta Kappan.* 753–761.

Green, Joseph. 1995. "Introduction to the Philosophical Remains of S. T. Coleridge." In *The Collected Works of Samuel Taylor Coleridge: Shorter Works and Fragments*, ed., H. J. Jackson and J. R. de J. Jackson, 1519–1536. Princeton, NJ: Princeton University Press.

Elam, Stanley M. 1993. "The 25th Annual Phi Delta Kappan/Gallup Poll." *Phi Delta Kappan.* 137–152.

Glasser, William. 1990. *The Quality School.* New York, NY: Harper Perennial.

"Guns Among Young People in the U.S." 1993. *Youth Record*, 3 August.

Jones, Clarrise. 1994. "Report Shows Violence Rising in Schools." *The New York Times*, 13 August.

Kozol, Jonathan. 1985. *Illiterate America.* Garden City, NY: Anchor Press/Doubleday.

Lawrence, Jerome, and Lee, Robert E. Inherit the Wind. In *Selected Plays of Jerome Lawrence and Robert E. Lee*, ed. Alan Woods, 9–68. Columbus, OH: The Ohio State University Press.

Merina, Anita. 1994. "Fighting School Violence Means Taking on Guns." *NEA Today*, 12 March.

National Commission on Excellence in Education. 1983. *A Nation at Risk*. Washington, DC: Department of Education.

Redfield, James. 1993. *The Celestine Prophecy*. New York, NY: Warner Books.

Rosenblatt, Louise. 1978. *The Reader, the Text, the Poem*. Carbondale, IL: Southern Illinois University Press.

Sagan, Carl, and Druyan, Ann. 1994. "Literacy—the Path to a More Prosperous, Less Dangerous America." *Parade Magazine*, 6 March.

Salinger, J.D. 1945. *The Catcher in the Rye*. New York, NY: Bantam Books.

Survey of the American Teacher. 1993. *Violence in America's Public Schools*. New York, NY: MetLife.

U.S. Bureau of the Census. 1979. "Literacy: Current Problems and Current Research." In *Fifth Report of the National Council on Educational Research*. Washington, DC: National Institute of Education.

Wellborn, Stanley. 1982. "A Nation of Illiterates?" *U.S. News and World Report*, 17 May.

Zimmer, Judith. 1993. *We Can Work It Out*. Culver City, CA: Social Studies School Service.

Chapter Three

Models for School Reform
The National Writing Project and Language Across the Curriculum

There's a tale about a popular professor whose former students were regularly hired to teach in local high schools. Several of her so-called "best-and-brightest" happened to be teaching in the same school, one known to be good, an award-winning school where all students were achieving at impressively high levels. This school had in place every current reform strategy imaginable: it had site-based management; it had whole language; it had language-across-the-curriculum; it had curriculum compression; it had authentic assessment; in collaboration with the local university college of education, it was a Professional Development School (PDS); it had team-planning, team-teaching, team-counseling; it had state-of-the-art technology; it had block scheduling; it had peer coaching; it had "schools-within-schools"—it had it all. The professor's former students kept dogging her to visit for a day to see just how good the school was because they were justifiably proud of it, but she was always too busy. Finally, after one last volley of invitations, the professor found time to accept. At the end of the day, the eager teachers rushed up to her and demanded, "Tell us, what do you think?" To which the professor replied, "Well, it looks good and it sounds good, but will it work in *theory*?"

The blending of theory and practice into coherent and effective approaches to schooling that works for everyone—adults included—is what marks enduring reform. A model we wish to endorse now, with all the requisite philosophy and conditions we have underscored thus far, is the National Writing Project, headquartered at the University of California, Berkeley, but with sites throughout the United States and some foreign countries. It began back in 1973 with twenty-five outstanding teachers in a summer institute, as the Bay Area Writing Project, which has since been replicated at more than 160 other sites. Basic assumptions of this exemplary model of school reform include the following, taken here from the *Virginia Writing Project: Model and Program Design* (1995, 2):

1. The university and the schools must work together as partners. The "top-down" tradition of past university-school programs is no longer acceptable as a faculty development model.

2. Successful teachers of writing can be identified, brought together during university summer institutes, and prepared to teach other teachers in follow-up programs in the schools.

3. Teachers are the best teachers of other teachers; successful practicing teachers have a credibility no outside consultant can match.

4. Summer institutes must involve teachers from all levels of instruction, elementary school through university; student writing needs constant attention from the early primary grades on through the university years.

5. Summer institutes must involve teachers from across the disciplines; writing is as fundamental to learning in science, in mathematics, and in history as it is in English and the language arts.

6. Teachers of writing must also write. Teachers must experience what they are asking of their students; the process of writing can be understood best by engaging in that process first hand.

7. Real change in classroom practice happens over time; effective staff development programs are ongoing and systematic, bringing teachers together regularly throughout their careers to test and evaluate the best practices of other teachers and the continuing development in the field.

8. What is known about the teaching of writing comes from research and from the practice of those who teach writing.

9. The National Writing Project, by promoting no single "right" approach to the teaching of writing, is now and will always be open to the best that is known about writing and the teaching of writing.

In National Writing Project sites, traditional lines that have separated school teachers and university professors are intentionally blurred. Teachers and professors, kindergarten through university, come together at a writing project site for four or five weeks each summer to share successes and problems and to collaborate on improving instruction. Teachers receive six graduate credit hours, tuition is typically paid by participating school districts, and teachers receive stipends upon completing the institute. To be selected, teachers submit written applications and consent to interviews. Eventually, twenty to twenty-five Fellows are selected each summer. Prior to the institute itself, teachers and project staff meet one or more times in the spring to get further acquainted and to orient one another to the summer's work. During the summer institute teachers read and write, respond to each other's reading and writing, and present sixty- to ninety-minute demonstration lessons from their classrooms, preceded by coaching and followed by rigorous critiques from fellow teachers. In this way, teachers literally train themselves to become *consultants* when they return to their schools in the fall. As teacher consultants, they share their knowledge with colleagues, and they are often paid to conduct workshops and seminars in their own and surrounding school districts.

When the National Writing Project began, it had three major goals according to founder James Gray, appearing on a PBS-sponsored videoconference at Robert Morris College, Pittsburgh, Pennsylvania, originally broadcast on February 24, 1994:

- improve the quality of teacher writing and instruction, as well as student writing
- improve the quality of faculty development
- empower classroom teachers

The Project, in the same videoconference, claims the following accomplishments:

- improved faculty development
- improved the teaching of writing
- extended language-across-the-curriculum
- broken barriers between research and teaching
- maintained an attitude of openness to "what works"

Evidence that the project *does* work—significant and concrete evidence—lies in many places. One notable piece of documentation, however, rests with this fact: it has regularly received corporate, foundation, local, state, and/or national funding during its entire twenty-five year history. Perhaps most telling is that it has received Congressional funding for nearly a decade. Its national funding level for 1996–1997 was nearly three million dollars, testimony to the per-

ception of its leadership, its committed teachers with near missionary zeal, and its bipartisan support in both houses of Congress. Over
200,000 teachers have attended Writing Project summer institutes
since 1974.

The following is a portion of an interview one of us (D.W.) conducted with James Gray, currently Chief Executive Officer of the
National Writing Project Corporation, for the *Slate Newsletter* (1–4)
of the National Council of Teachers of English, February 17, 1993.

D.W.: What must happen for significant educational reform to occur?

J.G.: To think of reform happening in a world of restructuring or reconsti-
tuting in which would-be reformers are not looking at what's happening in
classrooms and not inviting teachers to a major role as change agents—
that's never going to work. It never has worked. It's just more of the kind
of stuff we've had in the past. I don't want to suggest that what's happening now in reform movements is not necessarily teacher centered. There
are some indications that many of the different efforts are indeed responding more and more to teacher-power ideas, but nothing quite to the degree
that the National Writing Project has responded. The Writing Projects, as
you know, are university based, but they are very definitely teacher centered.

D.W.: What do you think is the role of legislation in educational reform?

J.G.: Simply put, legislation can support programs that are good. What leg-
islatures can do, because they're not academic centers, is take a broader
view of things, and be more open, perhaps, to the idea of teachers at the
center of reform. And this has happened. Basically, I think that reform
can't happen except through a model, such as the National Writing Project
model, that puts teachers at the center.

D.W.: Do you worry about legislators distorting the National Writing
Project model?

J.G.: No, not at all. We have found that some of the most careful supporters of our model are legislators and aides we have worked with. When we
came up with a new bill for the National Writing Project through the Congress, the aides that worked for us in the House and Senate were very sensitive to what they were saying in the legislation, and so every draft they
came up with came to us. They asked such questions as, Is this what teachers want? Will teachers like this? Is this O.K. for teachers? We haven't had
academics respond to it that way. We've had aides in Congress and in the
state houses respond to it that way.

D.W.: Do you think legislators are willing to be led by people who believe
they know what they're doing—like teachers?

J.G.: I wouldn't say it that way, but I think I know what you're getting at.
Yes, I do indeed. Particularly for programs like ours. When we started the
Bay Area Writing Project, we were trying to improve the writing of little
Republican kids as well as little Democratic kids. We were trying to serve

all schools and all teachers. That means all people, people that were yellow as well as white, or brown as well as black, or whatever. We were nonpolitical, apolitical. We're an umbrella to improve the nature of education in America for all schools, all teachers, all kids. Everybody is for that.

D.W.: And that hasn't changed?

J.G.: That hasn't changed. And because it's apolitical, it's one piece of legislation that Republicans and Democrats alike can cosponsor as they have done. It's one program that can go to committees and not create a hassle between the Democrats and Republicans. It's an example in Congress of a program that has a Democrat, George Miller, as cosponsor in the House and a Republican, Thad Cochran, as cosponsor in the Senate. The National Writing Project has received overwhelming bipartisan support in both houses of Congress.

D.W.: How have you been so successful with the Congress?

J.G.: What's interesting about this is that it almost seems accidental. It was Mississippi that led the charge for federal funding of the National Writing Project. It didn't do us any harm that the codirector of the Mississippi Writing Project was a close friend of Senator Thad Cochran. He had been impressed with what his daughter, Sherry, had been saying about the project, so he asked her to put together a package of material that would describe it, and after the Senator's next trip home, Sherry's father took the package to the airport to deliver it personally so that Senator Cochran could read it on the plane back to Washington. Cochran then gave the material to his education aide to look into. And this aide, who just happened to be an ex-student of the director of the Mississippi state project, recommended the project and arranged for a meeting with three or four of us in Washington. She recommended the project to the Senator, who also met with us. And soon after that meeting, Cochran told his aide, "Let's go for it!"

There is nothing more seductive than what works. Teachers are the best resources for enduring school reform, because they are able to share their successes and *show* what works. They discuss mutually felt problems and exchange ideas with colleagues at school sites where everyone has something immediately at stake every day. In such a climate of professional give and take, the model of outside consultants "blowing in, blowing off, and blowing out" has little place.

The message of the National Writing Project's success within many contexts is a lesson for school reform in general: significant and lasting change depends upon teachers who know what they're doing and can articulate why they're doing it; upon collegial relationships; upon including everybody; upon putting egos and us-versus-them attitudes aside; upon working hard every day and not giving up; and upon people striving openly together toward achieving common goals—teachers, administrators, policymakers, and politicians alike.

Teachers in any school are interested in students doing better work, as are legislators and everyone else. The teachers-teaching-teachers model of the National Writing Project, however, has a greater potential for achieving genuine school improvement than have models of the past. Simply put, significant school reform comes from the inside out, not the outside in. Inside out is the new model; outside in has had its day. The National Writing Project recognized that a long time ago. Current school reformers would do well to accept this new model as a treasured resource for those who would influence change.

Teachers as school reformers listen to their colleagues' voices with an empathetic spirit and a belief in everyone's desire to help children succeed in school. They respond to what they hear in civil, respectful ways, and they share what they learn from working with students in their own classrooms. They relate to colleagues as they relate to students: they ask questions, listen intently, share their own stories, demonstrate what works for them, constantly re-evaluate what they know and do, and—perhaps most crucially—possess an obstinate and obsessive faith. They help create teacher-centered schools as they create student-centered classrooms. This aim, spirit, and particular brand of dealing with others are the stuff of leadership, the catalyst for significant school reform.

As we write this, teachers from all sites of the National Writing Project throughout America are serving as catalysts for school reform. They are doing the work we are advocating. Many stories exist at every writing project site, but here are two examples. Terri Darnell and Karen Reidelbach are teachers in Virginia Beach, Virginia, and they are teacher consultants for the Tidewater Virginia Writing Project. They are experienced workshop and seminar leaders among their colleagues, and they work both individually and collaboratively. In their work with teachers, they do little preaching. Rather, in a typical series of workshop sessions (ten hours or more) they show teachers precisely how they spend every minute of every day in a typical week with students. They get teachers to experience many of the same learning activities that the two of them have found effective in their classrooms, and they invite teachers to tell their own stories. Terri and Karen are inquiry-oriented teachers of students and of other teachers. They open their classrooms to teachers' scrutiny. If a teacher says, "My students are not confident enough to make decisions about their own learning, as your students seem to be," Terri and Karen say, "We worried about the same thing, but once we took the risk, we were pleasantly surprised." They get good work from their students, and they show it to other teachers. Nothing is more per-suasive, more seductive and compelling, than classroom-based evidence. Their students produce good work because Terri and Karen expect good work and because they create an environment in which students develop confidence in their own abilities to succeed. Terri and Karen are effective leaders among their col-leagues, because they model excellent practice; they articulate theoretical and research-based support for that practice; they are open to learning from other teachers; and they continue to grow. So, too, do all teachers who take up the mantle of leadership and seize ownership of their profession.

Here's a letter Karen Reidelbach wrote on January 20, 1996 to the Tidewater Writing Project office.

> Terri and I just finished a job for the Hampton City Schools. It went well, as the evaluations show. Doing this work has become almost old-hat for Terri and me now. We've told the same stories a hundred times, but we still get energized by teachers we meet. The teachers in Hampton were excited and eager—ready to try new ideas, students' ideas, and teach in new and better ways. They were great! The job was refreshing and reminded me of when we got started.
>
> Anyway, watch out for some checks for us! We completed two ten-hour sessions, so each of us should receive $650.00. Also, Windsor Woods in Virginia Beach will be sending checks for a November job—$195.00 each for 6 hours.
>
> I'll be out of town for our next Writing Project continuity meeting. It seems I've had complications each time lately, and I feel that I'm barely doing anything for the Project. Here's a list of our jobs to show how the Project touches so many lives:

August, '95

Chesterfield County Schools	24 hrs.	80 people
Hampton City Schools	12 hrs.	180 people
Virginia Beach Schools	12 hrs.	40 people

September, '95

Virginia Beach Schools	10 hrs.	20 people

October, '95

Hampton City Schools	10 hrs.	40 people
Virginia Beach Schools	6 hrs.	30 people

January, '96

Hampton City Schools	10 hrs.	30 people

ON THE BOOKS

February, '96
Virginia Beach Schools   2 hrs.   30 people
(follow-up)

March, '96
State Reading Conference,   3 hrs.   (we've had 70 to
Norfolk   300 in past years)

Hope the meeting goes well. I'll call my delegate to support
continued funding for the Writing Project. It *has* changed my
teaching life.

The Writing Project has empowered Terri Darnell and Karen
Reidelbach as they have empowered it. They feel a keen sense of
professionalism as they work with other teachers to help students
grow. They possess credibility with their colleagues, because they
offer concrete proof that students succeed in their classrooms. They
are collegial; they share; they listen; they learn; they help; and they
lead. (Listen, learn, help, and lead—this is the formula for getting
things done promoted by Congressional House Speaker Newt Gingrich; seductive teachers know they can learn from anyone and everyone, if they maintain an attitude of openness.) Seductive
teachers seek to understand the deep-rooted cultures of their
schools as well as their classrooms. That is, they listen to the voices that define and describe the school culture created by their fellow faculty and administrators. As fully participating members of
that school culture, they learn to understand it. Then, and only
then, can they help to change it, if it needs changing.

A significant strand within the National Writing Project that further recommends it as a model for school reform is its advocacy of
language-across-the-curriculum. This is a movement in schools, we
submit, that is crucial for helping *all* teachers and students do better work. It is a British export, disseminated and developed over the
last two decades largely through National Writing Project sites. The
initial impetus for language-across-the-curriculum was provided by
the work of the late James Britton and his colleagues in England,
whose efforts in the mid-seventies gave the movement its force and
eventually propelled it across the Atlantic to America. Britton was
a distinguished scholar/teacher and faculty member at the University of London. His work with teachers on the connections that exist between language and learning has been profoundly influential.
In a 1978 address to teachers at Old Dominion University in Norfolk, Virginia, he offered the following:

An operational view of how students learn their Mother Tongue is that they must work to achieve something *else* through its use. They learn to get their own way through language by doing non-linguistic things with it. The satisfaction one gets from language use in school is the satisfaction of learning something else by means of language. The two are inextricably connected, language and learning.

From this, then, you get the campaign slogan of "Language across the Curriculum." We chose that—a group of English teachers in London who initiated this campaign which got caught up in the Bullock Report [the reference here is to Alan Bullock's *A Language for Life*, 1975, London: Her Majesty's Stationery Office—a study of language and learning in British schools]—because we thought it sounded American. What we wanted was a slogan with punch. So we tried it. We were criticized, when we applied for money to conduct a piece of research into it, by a headmistress of a comprehensive school in London, who said, "Surely you mean language throughout the curriculum!" It's a slogan—"Language across the Curriculum"—we need a slogan because what we're trying to do is interest teachers of physics and history and chemistry and geography and so on who don't know that language is their concern. We're trying to interest them in how language is working as an instrument of learning and help them to realize that language mastery in geography, for example, is being learned in geography lessons, not in English and then being applied in geography.

Let me give you one principle of what I mean by language for learning. I'm quoting from the *Bullock Report* now, in its early pages, "A child may learn as certainly by talking and writing as by listening and reading." This statement was ridiculed by the back to basics merchants in England. They all knew that children learn by reading a textbook and listening to the teacher. They also knew that children's talk was a waste of time and they can't write anyway.

What we said to them is that psycholinguistic views of recent years suggest clearly that in order to take information from a text or teacher, a student has to go through a process quite like finding out for himself or herself. In order to accept new information, we have to have somewhere to put it. Having somewhere to put it means possessing a vast network of knowledge and experience into which the new information fits in such a way as to make links. And if it doesn't make links we can't take it in. . . . The student's own language provides those links to learning, even while reading and listening. . . .

Each school subject's special language often presents the first obstacle for many students to conquer. Language, then, is every teacher's business, not just the English teacher's. Students must actively use the language of different subject areas to gain control of those subject areas. The classroom, however, must be a safe arena in which students learn to care about mastering subject matter, as well as the language that makes such mastery possible. This process is gradual and developmental. Students bring to school language experiences that range from a mastery of standard American English, to English as a second language, to "street" language, to "hip" language, to slang, and so on. That is, students bring to school many varieties of language use, many dialects. Seductive teachers know that all these forms of the English language must be admitted into the classroom if students are to benefit fully from what the classroom has to offer. To deny the languages and experiences that students bring in is to deny their only present instruments for learning.

Teaching itself is a powerful way of learning. Ask any seductive teacher. The quickest route to finding out how much you know about something is to try to teach it to someone else. Teachers find out in their first year of teaching—sometimes first day—what they don't know well enough to teach. If we are right about the power of *teaching* as a *learning* process, then doesn't it stand to reason that classrooms should be places where students regularly play the role of teachers? Humming, productive classrooms are often places where students are teaching students, and teachers are serving as guides, resources, planners, and careful observers. To state the matter theatrically, the teacher is setting the stage and working the lights.

As a seductive teacher attempts to communicate with students, he or she is always on the lookout for signals that students are actively trying to make meaning. Students say things like, "In other words . . ."; or "Are you saying that . . ."; or "Do you mean . . ."; or "Are you telling me . . ."; or "What I hear you saying is . . ."; or "Are you suggesting . . ." Utterances such as these tell seductive teachers that students are actively listening and attempting to "understand." The longer teachers talk to students, however, without expecting or inviting responses, the less likely it is that teachers are *teaching*. What they are doing is *telling*. Seductive teachers know that they can tell thirty students something, but only a few of them are told. Teaching, obviously, requires communicating. Communicating in a classroom, as elsewhere, is a matter of *negotiating* meaning. Language is the medium for this negotiation. Teachers who are interested in communicating ideas and information to students as clearly and as accurately as possible know that communicating demands negotiating. All parties involved must actively participate in the process—that is, they must all *use* language, *produce* it, and *exchange* it back and forth to achieve anything close to a common understanding, to a tight interpretive community.

In fact, seductive teachers use language and elicit it from students as a way of acknowledging and extending the interpretive communities of their classrooms. Interpretive communities may be tight or loose. Tight ones share similar views of their worlds, and loose ones may hold wildly dissimilar views. Professor Stanley Fish, of Duke University, suggests what happens in tight interpretive communities by describing two classes of graduate students he once taught back-to-back. During the first class, he wrote on the board the names of several linguists as follows (1980, 323):

Jacobs—Rosenbaum
                    Levin
                    Thorne
                    Hayes
                    Ohman (?)

(The question mark means he wasn't sure of the spelling.) When his next class came in, a group who had been reading seventeenth-century religious poetry, Fish told them that on the board was a religious poem. He asked them to interpret it; and, indeed, they interpreted it as a religious poem! Fish says, "Jacobs was explicated as a reference to Jacob's ladder, traditionally allegorized as a figure for the Christian ascent to heaven," and so on (324).

Seductive teachers realize that individual perceptions and world views in classrooms are transported there by students' past experiences. Teachers acknowledge and respect those experiences but attempt to extend them to create a special community (learning environment) that values school. In such a community, meaning is negotiated by means of language, everybody's language. Whether working with students or with colleagues, seductive teachers acknowledge the possible existence of "loose" interpretive communities but attempt to tighten them by helping to create a climate in which everybody has similar expectations and goals (such as to do better work, as a good starting place). In such a climate and community as this, everyone speaks, everyone listens, and new meanings emerge.

Teachers as school reformers facilitate negotiating, and through negotiating, healthy change is possible, in both classrooms and faculty gathering places. Is it too much to hope for the following? What if a school's faculty were to become the kind of tight interpretive community that sees every classroom full of students the same way—as interesting, growing human beings who, regardless of the baggage they bring in, can be reached and can be taught to achieve at high levels? A goal of English teachers as reformers might be to help create such tight communities of faculty members in their schools. Amazing things could happen.

In short, how students use language in classrooms and how seductive teachers encourage and value that language significantly influence learning. The same is true for communication among colleagues. Teachers, deciding to lead school reform, know that all voices must be heard and respected. Such teachers listen to other teachers; they learn; they help; and they lead (Newt Gingrich's mantra again). As we have said, seductive teachers know they can (even must) learn from anyone and everyone, regardless of the interpretive community to which one belongs. It is this mutual learning that is the genesis of authentic school reform, and seductive teachers act on that awareness.

Essential to the success of teaching and learning is the way teachers themselves use, encourage, and allow language. Language is a fundamental—perhaps *the* fundamental—medium for teaching and learning in school. It is a principle vehicle by which people conceptualize and attempt to convey meaning, make sense, and express feelings. Being able to use language that truly communicates is a "ticket" into the social conversation that learning and literacy require.

As Sylvia Ashton-Warner, celebrated teacher and writer from New Zealand, wrote over three decades ago, "Helen Keller's first word, 'water,' was a one-word book" (1963, 27). When Helen Keller, blind and deaf, "cracked the code" of language and realized its connection to the world she desperately wanted and needed to understand, she was off and running. The rest is history, so to speak. So it is with every student, less sensational perhaps, but essentially the same.

There's a story about a seminary student about to flunk out of school. He had to take a course in which he could make an A if he was going to survive. His classmates advised him to sign up for whatever Professor Smith was teaching, because he always gave the same exam question, "Trace the missionary journeys of Paul." So the student did and, with his classmates, spent the entire semester preparing for that question. When exam day came, the old professor strolled into the lecture hall and wrote this directive on the chalkboard, "Write a critical analysis of the Sermon on the Mount." Everybody nearly swooned except for the desperate student who wrote and wrote until the end of the exam period. When grades were posted several days later, everyone saw that this student had made an A, while everyone else had failed. His classmates gathered around to see what he had written. What they saw was this, "Let those who will, criticize the Master. As for me, I shall trace the missionary journeys of Paul." Our point is, as seductive teachers know, writing succeeds when the writer has something to say. As a corollary, learning succeeds when the learner has something to learn, that is, when the learner finds a personal reason to learn.

Here's another illustration of this point. Several years ago we were teaching a course on "Language for Learning Across the Curriculum" in a nearby school district, every Wednesday evening for fifteen weeks. One of the teachers taking the course was a basketball coach who also taught remedial reading. Every week as he came to class he muttered something about how he didn't think he could use this "stuff" in his remedial reading class. He said this so often that we, too, began to worry. During the last few sessions, each teacher was to report for fifteen to twenty minutes on how he or she was using language-across-the-curriculum in the classroom. When the time came for the teacher/coach to speak, we couldn't wait to hear what he had to say. (We felt he couldn't wait to hear what he had to say, as well.)

> I have a third-period remedial reading class of students who, for the whole year, were always passing notes to one another. But they didn't know that I knew they were doing that. One morning, about a month ago, I walked into class and said, "Take everything off your desks but a sheet of paper and a pencil. I want you to find someone in this class that you have *not* written a note to! Write a note to that person, and when you get your note, write back. But be careful what you say because I'm going to collect the notes and redistribute them so that you do not get your own. And we're going to use these notes as our reading lesson for today."
>
> The students were startled, but they did what I said. And it worked! Students attended to their reading lessons longer and better than they ever had before. So I kept doing this, and it kept working. Then yesterday I was sitting in the teachers' lounge late in the afternoon, and the toughest English teacher in the school came in and sat beside me. She's the type who can spot a comma splice across a football field!
>
> This is what she told me, "I don't know what you're doing in your third-period remedial reading class, but I have some of your students in my fourth-period English class. I gave them an assignment to pick their favorite writer they had read this year and write an essay to say why they chose whom they chose. *And Sally picked Johnny from your third-period remedial reading class!* Johnny beat out Shakespeare, Milton, Wordsworth, Byron, Shelley, and Keats!"

> We had a big laugh over this, but I'll have to admit I was
> proud! What I want to know is—what happened?

So what did happen in this teacher's classroom? Whatever it was happened somewhat by accident, because he and his students stumbled across something that worked in a most interesting way. Other teachers in our class that Wednesday night discussed his report and concluded several things. First, what he had used was a "language experience" approach to teaching reading. The language experience approach assumes that students are more interested in their own language than they are in someone else's; therefore, they are likely to attend to that language far longer and more intently than they are likely to attend to a textbook writer's language. That is partly what happened in his classroom. Something else happened, however, perhaps of greater significance: students came to see themselves as *real* writers and readers, not just students of writing and reading. That recognition kept them going, kept them reading, writing, and growing.

Seductive teachers know that if they can get students to see themselves more as *practitioners* than mere *students* of their subjects, then the classroom learning environment is vigorously healthy. It is not exaggerating to say that when students learn to behave as real writers and readers (or mathematicians or scientists or historians), teachers can almost FAX their lesson plans to school each day and stay home to work in the garden. Under such conditions, equipped with self-directed attitudes toward themselves, students come to class ready to produce—and produce, they do. It's also not too much of a stretch to say the same about teachers. When teachers are invited to speak their minds, when they are heard, valued, and respected in terms of their own experience, they accomplish more. They acquire a greater sense of self-efficacy. Sometimes they change their thinking, their perspective, and their teaching practice. So we'll repeat; *teachers as school reformers help create the same collegial climate in their schools as they do in their classrooms.*

In effective teachers' classrooms, language use is a matter of "social behavior." Teachers and students concern themselves with the "etiquette" of language, with what is appropriate in given situations. The usage one chooses and the stance one takes—in speech or in writing—always depend upon the demands of a particular occasion, as do the clothes one selects to wear for a particular event or function. As students begin to grasp these attitudes and understandings about language, they begin to see the value of learning standard English, as well as a subject area's particular jargon. They perceive a need to know and to be able to use an unfamiliar language because it gives them more versatility and power—*reward*—as they move across an ever-widening academic and social spectrum.

We'll offer one more example of a National Writing Project teacher working as a school reformer, a near legendary teacher of teachers among those who know him. "Know your stuff; love your kids; be a professional"—these are the words of Bob Tierney, for more than twenty years a biology teacher at Irvington High School in Fremont, California. They are words that might well become the motto of seductive teachers everywhere.

For many years Tierney was an excellent "traditional" teacher of tenth-grade biology. Later in his career, however, he attended a five-week summer institute of the Bay Area Writing Project at U.C., Berkeley, the original site of what is now known as the National Writing Project. The only science teacher in a room filled with English teachers, Tierney says, "All summer long, I dared not use either *who* or *whom*." After that institute, in which excellent teachers came together to demonstrate their successes and share their problems, Tierney began to experiment with innovative ways of teaching that excited both him and his students—in ways that improved their learning of biology.

For much of his teaching life, Tierney taught biology the way most adults tend to remember it from their own high schools days.

1. a reading assignment, usually a chapter
2. a "stimulating" lecture about the topic
3. a lab designed to reinforce what he told students in the lecture
4. a follow-up of the lab, usually a review sheet or lab workbook exercise
5. a multiple-choice test

Writing about his teaching in those days, Tierney says

> My lessons were entirely teacher-generated, teacher-motivated, and teacher-owned. It was a safe, comfortable method of presenting information. My lesson plans indicated I would cover certain concepts of science and the workbooks verified that I did, indeed, present the material—sort of education by checklist. It was boring. I looked forward to retirement. (1983, 9)

After a period of experimentation, however, Tierney came upon what he now calls "almost entirely student-owned lessons" (9).

In the later stages of his development as a teacher, he began to teach biology according to the following general sequence:

1. Ascertain what the students already understand by having each of them write down one or two things they know about the sub-

ject, and then poll the class (for example, in beginning a unit on photosynthesis, the teacher might say, "How do plants get food? Write down some guesses").

2. After some oral discussion of what students write, ask students to formulate one or two questions they really want answered.

3. Give short reading assignments that require students to write in response to their reading.

4. Set up a lab that lends itself to genuine student investigation, and do not answer any questions during the lab. Require, instead, students to write any questions they have on their lab papers.

5. After students have indicated their questions, outline a lecture to respond to the questions.

6. During the lecture, pause about every ten minutes to allow students to respond (by both talking and writing) to what is being said in the lecture.

7. Assign homework that requires writing-to-think activities.

8. Conclude the unit with a short essay test.

Tierney says he has learned to vary the audiences for whom students write. Sometimes they write for other students; other times he places posters on the wall of X, Y, or Z familiar celebrity and asks students to explain things to them. "By changing the posters," Tierney writes, "I can change audience, thus forcing the student to look at the topic from a different perspective" (9). Did more of their own talk and writing help students learn biology better? Tierney claims, "I undertook to test whether biology students retained what they learned better [from these new ways of teaching]. The results left no doubts—they did. He further testifies, "I have been converted from a dispenser of information to a facilitator of learning. I teach science as a process. . . . My teaching is more effective and a lot more fun" (9). Finally, he acknowledges English teachers' impact on his work—particularly the influence of his colleague at Irvington High School, Keith Caldwell, himself a master English teacher. Tierney writes, ". . . I am grateful . . . to my colleagues who teach English. . . . Maybe I will take an English teacher to lunch tomorrow and steal a few more good ideas" (9).

Bob Tierney became a researcher/innovator in his own classroom, relentlessly pursuing more effective ways to teach and testing the results. Furthermore, he became a teacher of other teachers, a "teacher's teacher." Over the last decade, he has conducted scores of workshops and seminars for other teachers—teachers of both science and other subject areas—all across America and abroad. In these workshops and seminars, he describes his own teacher growth, his beliefs as a master teacher, and the details of his own classroom experiences. Bob Tierney represents untold numbers of seductive teachers who *must seize or be given the charge and opportunity to work side by side with their colleagues if lasting school reform is to take hold.*

Through the National Writing Project, Bob Tierney accepted the charge and opportunity to participate in his colleagues' growth. Many other seductive teachers, in a grass-roots way, are meeting the same challenge in nearly all fifty states today. Education reform movements must embrace these teachers and support their efforts in every way possible. This kind of curricular reform is what must be facilitated and supported by administrative, policy, and funding reform. Policy, funding, and administrative reform may precede school reform, but it does not make it happen.

Those who shape policy, allocate funds, and establish administrative processes and procedures can never reform schools, except cosmetically. They can only reform the system and climate in which schooling occurs. But that will be sufficient. Then the baton passes to teachers; only they can do the reforming. They must decide to lead. The model that will work, finally, is a teachers-teaching-teachers model—confident, able teachers working with their colleagues to create high-quality schools.

References

Ashton-Warner, Sylvia. 1963. *Teacher.* New York, NY: Simon and Schuster.

"Basic Assumptions." 1995. *Virginia Writing Project: Model and Program Design.* Fairfax, VA: Northern Virginia Writing Project.

Britton, James. 1978. Address to invited teachers, August 15, at Old Dominion University, Norfolk, VA.

Fish, Stanley. 1980. *Is There a Text in This Class?* Cambridge, MA: Harvard University Press.

Gray, James. 1993. "An Interview with James Gray." Interview by Denny Wolfe. *SLATE Newsletter* 18 (1): 1–5.

Gray, James. 1994. "Writing Across the Curriculum: How Schools, Colleges and Communities Collaborate to Improve Learning, Part 2." Pittsburgh, PA: PBS Adult Learning Satellite Service/Robert Morris College, 24 February (videoconference).

Tierney, Bob. 1983. "Writing in Science." *California English Teacher* 19 (2): 8–9.

Chapter Four

The Subject/Object Factor

In considering the "subject/object factor," we want to elaborate on why teachers must decide to lead school reform and what empowers them to do so. We also want to revisit the concept of curriculum in light of how the best teachers tend to view it, as opposed to how others tend to view it.

When one approaches a problem—particularly a formidable one like school reform—perception is everything. That is to say, one must truly believe that something can be done to improve the situation; otherwise, nothing of consequence *will* be done. Without a sense that conditions can truly be improved, so-called solutions will be merely cosmetic, resulting from political motivations to give the appearance that "we're doing something" even if that "something" really doesn't help teachers and kids do better work. So whose perceptions count most? We believe that in school reform, as in other things, the perceptions that count most belong to those who are closest to the problem—closest to understanding it and closest to knowing what the solutions are. In the case at hand, those closest to the problems of schools are teachers, particularly where issues of student learning are concerned.

In any organization—whether it's a school, a business, or a civic club—there are at least two kinds of workers: *leaders* and *followers*. We acknowledge the modesty of this division, but we believe it is apt; there are those who *act* (subject) and there are those who are *acted upon* (object). Regarding schools, there are teachers who struggle through each day, just trying to "keep the lid on." They know conditions are bad, but they're "doing the best we can." Such teachers engage in a lot of avoidance behaviors: they avoid dealing with troubled youth, feeling it's best just to leave them alone; they avoid exploring new ways to teach because the old ones are comfortable (and the new ones "wouldn't work for our kids, anyway"); they avoid deep involvement with students and parents in "extra-class" relationships because they feel their jobs begin and end with the starting and closing bells of each class period; and they see their curriculum as a static thing, which some students will "get" and others will not because "that's the way school is." About students, they are often heard to utter statements like, "I don't know why they didn't get it. I went *over* it and *over* it and *told* them and *told* them. What more can I do? It's there if they want it."

While we may be describing the extreme case here, we know and you know it exists. Such teachers as we are describing tend to see themselves as victims—not bad people, but generally powerless. They are victims of forces they believe they are unable to defeat or even confront, such as unmotivated students, unappreciative administrators, and negligent parents. In some cases, they may be right on each count, but they feel unable to cope with the situation. They feel acted upon as innocent "objects," so they trudge along, "doing the best we can," with little conviction that they can truly make a difference in the grand scheme of things.

There are other teachers out there, though, seductive ones, who also struggle. They, however, are not interested merely in "keeping the lid on"; they are interested in "making the pot boil." They, too, know conditions are bad, but they question whether they're "doing the best we can." Such teachers are reflective practitioners of the art and science of teaching. They know the value of self-assessment; they are sensitive to the daily dynamics that operate within their classroom cultures; and they use what they learn from those dynamics to make their classrooms more accommodating and hospitable to all. Equipped with new and revised understandings that they earn through hard and focused work, these teachers make adjustments and sometimes change course entirely; they find and use strategies that work better in helping students learn.

Master teachers engage in a lot of "encounter" behaviors. They encounter troubled youth and attempt to help them cope. They encounter new ways to teach and carefully consider them as possibilities for reaching students more fully than before. They encounter students and parents in "extra-class" activities because they feel their jobs include building relationships and partnerships in the total school community, not just inside their own classrooms. They see their curriculum as fluid, not static, a curriculum that is possible for all students to "get." About students, they are often heard to say things like, "The kids didn't get it today. I've got to think about why. I'm going to talk it over with them tomorrow and find out what's going on." These kinds of teachers exist, too. We know it, and we hope you're lucky enough to know it. Maybe you are one.

Master teachers tend to see themselves as inquirers, decision-makers, and problem solvers (subjects)—the same traits they wish their students to acquire. They tend not to see themselves as victims (objects). They feel capable of pursuing solutions to school problems. They act according to what their preparation, intuition, reason, and/or experience have taught them. So they keep pushing and growing, knowing that they (as well as their students and colleagues) can do better—and that *maybe* none of us are yet doing "the best we can."

One way to illustrate the differences we are describing—the differences between some teachers (objects) and master teachers (subjects)—is through the following story. It involves two anthropologists. It seems that the first anthropologist entered a primitive tribal village and found its inhabitants huddled together, quaking in fear. Naked and screaming, they were pointing to an object in a nearby field and calling it a "monster." To get a closer look, the anthropologist walked into the field and saw that the object was not a monster at all. It was a giant watermelon. So the anthropologist returned to the villagers, shaking his head and chuckling to himself as he approached them. He lectured the villagers this way, "No-no, you don't understand. That object in the field is not a monster. Your fear is groundless. The thing you are fearful of is just a watermelon, a giant gourd. You can cut it open and eat it. Its pulp is cool and juicy and delicious to the taste," rubbing his stomach and licking his lips as he spoke his final words. The villagers killed him.

The next day another anthropologist—a seductive one—entered the village. He found the same scene—villagers huddled together, quaking in fear, pointing to an object in the field and calling it a "monster." This anthropologist also walked into the field and found that the object was not a monster but a watermelon. Unlike the first one, however, he drew his machete, chopped the watermelon into bits and pieces, and hurled the scraps into the forest. He then pounded his chest and returned to the villagers. They made him king. Over time, he was able to teach them the difference between a monster and a watermelon.

Like some teachers, the first anthropologist depended strictly upon explanation to educate the villagers—teaching as mere telling. If they just knew the "truth," he reasoned, the villagers would be set free. Unfortunately for him, his strategy backfired. The second anthropologist knew better. He knew he must acknowledge the villagers' "truth" before they would ever be likely to acknowledge his. The second anthropologist knew—as seductive teachers know—that the process of education is slow and gradual. It depends largely upon *building relationships* and *trust* with those to be taught. It means leading, attracting, and winning over people to a willingness to learn, to see anew, to become part of a fresh community. Learning itself is often the easy part, after one really feels safe, respected, and wants to do it.

Yet another way to describe the differences between some teachers and seductive ones is to consider each in light of the terms *classic* and *romantic*. This is a more academic way to approach the matter, but for some, perhaps a richer one, yielding insight into why the differences exist in the first place. Characteristics often assigned to a classic outlook include reason, logic, order, laws, rules, objectivity, and control. (Does this sound like the first anthropologist?) Characteristics assigned to a romantic outlook include intuition, imagination, resistance to order and rules, subjectivity, and spontaneity. (We do not claim that these describe the second anthropologist.)

In his book *Zen and the Art of Motorcycle Maintenance*, Robert Pirsig deals obsessively with these two terms. He distinguishes between them this way.

> "A classic understanding sees the world primarily as underlying form. . . . A romantic understanding sees it primarily in terms of immediate appearance. . . . The romantic mode is primarily inspirational . . . intuitive. . . . Feelings rather than facts predominate. . . .
>
> The classic mode, by contrast, proceeds by reason and by laws. . . . Although motorcycle *riding* is romantic, motorcycle *maintenance* is purely classic." (1974, 61)

When we apply classic and romantic labels to the act of teaching, we can subdivide nonseductive teachers accordingly: purely classic and purely romantic.

The purely classic group insists upon order, laws, and rules dominating the classroom at all times. When students do not conform, classic teachers are thrown off balance; such behavior defies their sense of logic. In their purely objective ways of viewing the world, they have trouble fathoming why a student might sleep in class, cut school, hit (cut/shot) another student, fail to do homework, or solve a problem by a means different from that prescribed in a textbook.

Classic teachers insist upon control, and they have little or no tolerance for ambiguity and nonconformity. Certainty and predictability are values that drive classic teachers' views of the world, as well as their approaches to teaching. Many school administrators and parents admire classic teachers. Their classrooms are often free of noise and commotion; every year they "cover the curriculum" from beginning to end; their assignments to students are detailed and orderly; they are "neat," and they expect students to be "neat"; they always are punctual; their classes begin on time and end on time; they always can be counted on to turn in reports to the office correctly and legibly. School custodians love them. Students may think of them as "hard." Classic teachers own their classrooms and maintain them just as classic motorcycle owners maintain their machines.

On the other side is the "romantic" bunch. Purely romantic teachers run what often seems to be chaotic classrooms. If any order or rules exist, they are rarely apparent. Students seem to come and go as they please, and the romantic teacher isn't particularly bothered by these events. Purely romantic teachers almost never "cover the curriculum" in sequence from beginning to end. They tend to operate spontaneously in their classrooms, allowing students to get them "off track" to deal with whatever students themselves wish to deal with. Romantic teachers have faith in their students, to be sure, an optimistic belief that students can and will succeed. Such teachers are interested primarily in the "feeling" lives of students, holding tight to the view that self-esteem is a necessary precursor to success of any positive kind.

There is, however, a "dark side" to the psyche of romantic teachers. They often despair and fret over students who too often are unsuccessful. Their "hearts go out" to such students, and they attempt to empathize mightily. Purely romantic teachers place a high value on students' efforts to succeed, whether or not those efforts result in achievement according to school "standards," which are esteemed by classic teachers. Many students admire romantic teachers, while thinking of them as "easy." Administrators and parents often see them as "loose cannons." Students like the freedom they are allowed in romantic teachers' classrooms. They know such teachers are "there" when they need them, no matter what. They know they can take creative liberties with assignments. They know it's generally O.K. to turn in homework and papers late. On tests, they know their pure opinion will be valued in equal measure with factual knowledge. They know romantic teachers are their friends. School custodians dread entering romantic teachers' classrooms. Like a romantic cyclist who values the ride over maintaining the machine, a romantic teacher values the journey with students over maintaining the conventional concept of *curriculum*.

By now you may be saying to yourself, "Hold on. Are these guys serious? Can teachers really be divided into such extreme camps as these?" To that we answer yes and no. While we have described pure classic-oriented teachers and pure romantic-oriented teachers in their extremes, we are aware of the trouble with a word like *pure*. As a concept, *pure* is a rare and precious descriptor. Certainly, such teachers as we have described exist. We have known them, and maybe you have, too; but, they are not typical. Most teachers we branded as "other" teachers or "nonseductive" teachers are neither purely classic nor purely romantic, of course. The kinds of teachers we are talking about, however, do have sharp leanings more toward the classic than the romantic, or more toward the romantic than the classic. Our main point is this: there does exist a basic orientation to teaching—as to anything else—that might be described as either classic or romantic, as objective or subjective. The former tends to emphasize what; the latter, who.

The classic-oriented teacher is usually a team player, one who respects and values the school as "system," though not always happy with it. The romantic-oriented teacher is a bit of a maverick, often critical of the school as system and often ignoring or challenging its rules. If there is ever a rational conflict between the school and the student, the classic-oriented teacher can be predicted to side with the school; the romantic-oriented teacher, with the student. (As an example, if an eleventh-grade student petitions a teacher to read a book for "credit" that is not on the school-approved list, the classic-oriented teacher will likely refuse the student's petition on that ground only—that it is not on the list. Given the same scenario, the romantic-oriented teacher will likely champion the student's right over the school's right to select a book.) Before moving on to a characterization of master teachers in light of the dichotomy and tension we have drawn between classic and romantic oriented teachers, we think it is necessary to say a few words about the school curriculum.

You already have, of course, your own conception of what *curriculum* means in its barest sense—the courses of study offered by a school, perhaps. But what of the curriculum's purpose? We think there is still a fair amount of agreement in America about purposes of the school curriculum, fragile though this agreement might be. It seems to us relatively safe to say that most thoughtful Americans generally agree on what the school curriculum is for: it's to help students learn to read, write, talk, listen, view, and think at the "highest possible levels" according to their individual abilities. Further, it's to help students understand and use such subjects as mathematics, science, technology, and history to function as responsible citizens in a democracy. We believe that the majority of Americans have little fundamental disagreement with those purposes as we have stated them (although there may be many different interpretations given to phrases like "highest possible levels," "individual abilities," and "responsible citizens").

After these broad-stroke agreements regarding purposes, however, the matter of curriculum becomes both complicated and controversial. What should students read? What should they write and talk about? To what and whom should they listen? What films should they view? What science should they study? What technology will they use? Whose version(s) of history should they learn? Answers to such questions go beyond the scope of this book. Let us observe, however, as textbook writers and editors tend to say, that "answers will vary," depending on agreements worked out among the constituents of each community a school serves. Heated arguments continue to rage over such questions as these, in both academia and the society at large, and the arguments will go on.

In the end, though, such questions are unanswerable in any broad sense; the answers will always be relative. But the general purposes of a school curriculum seem still intact—to help students learn to read, write, talk, listen, and view; to help them understand and use mathematics, science, and history; to help them learn to think (questionable?); to help them function responsibly in a democracy. (If you think those purposes no longer exist, you may not be wrong; but, we believe seductive teachers and thoughtful citizens still acknowledge and embrace them. It is, perhaps, their romantic side at work, as well as ours.)

What we wish to suggest now, however, is that there is something else about the school curriculum that is ignored all too often, lost in the other debates: the student. Irony of ironies. We wish to argue that students are a *part* of the curriculum, not just its *targets*. Students must be viewed in this way in any significant school reform effort. In extreme cases, classic teachers tend to think of the curriculum strictly as a what (the courses of study); romantic teachers tend to think of it as a who (the students themselves). Master teachers, on the other hand, know that the curriculum is both a what and a who—that is to say, it is classic and romantic at the same time. (Our second anthropologist knew that, also: he had a what to teach, but he had a whom to teach, and he knew he had to deal with both simultaneously. The villagers were part of the watermelon, and it was part of them.)

Of course, the curriculum is English, mathematics, science, and so on; but, it is also the learner. Seductive teachers know they must connect the what of the curriculum with the who of the classroom. In other words, the experiences students bring with them to school must be integrated with the curriculum that awaits them there. Seductive teachers know they can't just implant the content into the student without putting the student into the content. They know they must create a simultaneity of classic and romantic worlds in their classrooms—not two coexisting worlds but one world. Seductive teachers, therefore, are always working on the problem of student motivation in the following way: finding out how to integrate the "stuff" of the paper curriculum with the "stuff" of students' lives.

Let us try to explain what we mean more precisely, as we focus now on what really makes master teachers tick, on what separates them from the purely classic-oriented teachers and the purely romantic-oriented teachers. To help with this, we think it is useful to come back to Robert Pirsig's *Zen and the Art of Motorcycle Maintenance.*

Pirsig himself explains the surprising, immense success of his best-selling book by calling it a "culture-bearer" (376). A culture-bearing book, he claims, occurs almost accidentally. It appears at a time when the culture itself is already changing in the same direction that the book illuminates—*Uncle Tom's Cabin*, for example, appearing at a time when the culture was already rejecting slavery. *Zen*, Pirsig argues, appeared at a time (early 70s) when U.S. culture was rejecting the traditional American Dream: material success as the only road to happiness. He says this about his book, "It's . . . an expansion of the meaning of 'success' to something larger than just getting a good job and staying out of trouble" (377). He suggests that the book offers another kind of goal to work toward: finding peace of mind through capturing a sense of wholeness within yourself. It is this sense of "wholeness" that master teachers value and work toward, in themselves and in their students.

In *Zen*, Pirsig is on a cross-country journey by motorcycle with his young son, Chris. Along the way he engages in many philosophical meditations about different ways of viewing the world, through both his own voice and that of "Phaedrus," the name he gives his "old self" (destroyed by now illegal, involuntary, electroshock treatment when Pirsig was in a mental institution). In the course of long (some would say tedious) analyses of differences between romantic and classic modes of knowing, Pirsig arrives at the conclusion that these views, in and of themselves, are insufficient. So he posits something he calls Quality as a synthesis of the two. A common scholarly criticism of *Zen* is that Pirsig never fully develops just what Quality is. Here, however, are some things he does say about it.

1. . . . even though Quality cannot be defined, *you know what Quality is!* (185)

2. A real understanding of Quality *captures* the System, tames it, and puts it to work for one's own . . . use. (200)

3. Quality is not *objective*. . . . It doesn't reside in the material world. . . . Quality is not *subjective*. . . . It doesn't reside merely in the mind. . . . Quality is a *third* entity. . . . (213)

4. Quality is not a *thing*. It is an event. (215)

5. Believe me, when the world is seen not as a duality of mind and matter but as a trinity of *quality, mind*, and *matter*, then the art of motorcycle maintenance and other arts take on a dimension of meaning they never had. (221)

6. Quality [is] the source and substance of everything. (226)

7. If you want to build a factory, or fix a motorcycle, or set a nation right without getting stuck, then classical, structured dualistic subject-object knowledge, although necessary, isn't enough. You have to have some feeling for the *quality* of the work. . . . It's not just "intuition," . . . . not just "skill." . . . It's the direct result of contact with basic *reality*, Quality. . . . (255)

8. Both classic and romantic understandings of Quality must be combined. (262)

[If Pirsig has not defined *Quality* to any reader's satisfaction, no one else seems to have done much better.] In several dictionaries we consulted about *Quality*, one word appears regularly in the definitions: *excellence*—more of a synonym than a definition, and just as abstract. William Glasser, in *The Quality School*, offers this, "It would be extremely difficult to come up with an exact definition of quality education that would apply to all situations. *Even without being able to define it, however, we can almost always recognize quality when we see it*" (6). While none of this exonerates Pirsig from scholarly criticism, it at least magnifies the size of the task: Quality is one of those slippery concepts, perhaps impossible to pin down totally.

Zen has a happy ending, by the way. About four pages from the end of the book Chris asks his father (Pirsig), "Were you really insane?" The answer comes back crisply, "No!" With Chris as a final catalyst, Phaedrus (his old self) and Pirsig (the here and now self) become integrated. Pirsig is "whole." A Quality event has occurred: the "classic" motorcycle mechanic and the "romantic" motorcycle rider have become one. The subject/object duality has been resolved—Phaedrus (the acted upon) and Pirsig (the current actor) have merged in a Quality moment. Pirsig's quest, for now, has reached a destination.

We have used a fair amount of space on *Zen and the Art of Motorcycle Maintenance*. We're trying to underscore and to illustrate the complexity, difficulty, and splendor of what teachers must accomplish to become truly seductive. They must break away from the old bonds of classic and romantic views of teaching to become something else, to become "whole," if they are to do their work as well as it can be done.

Let us try to be precise about this. Seductive teachers know that while control (classic) is important in a classroom, so is freedom (romantic); that while the object (classic) of the curriculum must be honored, so must the subject of the curriculum, the student (romantic); that while teachers must be models of order, logic, and organization (classic) for students, they must be empathetic (romantic) when students fall short; that while they must respect, value, and maintain school rules and standards (classic), they must champion students' causes (romantic); they know that while facts (classic) are important, so are students' opinions (romantic). And—perhaps most telling—they know that parts do not always add up to wholes—i.e., Quality with a capital Q.

Teachers become seductive when they integrate subjective and objective ways of viewing their jobs into a whole. It's not a matter of leaning one way or another, toward the classic or the romantic, and it's not just a matter of balance. It's a matter of genuine integration of these dualistic ways of viewing and inventing classrooms and schools.

Subject and object are equally valid, but only as components of a whole. To achieve Quality, seductive teachers know that "truth" is a twin, that effective teaching means bringing about a harmonious relationship between the school and the community, between colleague and colleague, between student and student, between the subjects to be learned and the learners to be taught. Teaching and learning, for example, become one. When this occurs you have a Quality School.

Another quick story on this point. A linguistics professor was lecturing his class on the history of the double negative. He traced it through Elizabethan times when the double negative was standard. He noted that while two negatives make a positive, in no case can two positives make a negative. To which a student in the back of the room responded, "Yeah, right." (Is there any "truth" upon which we can depend?) Master teachers, we believe, tend not to think in polarities; they tend to resist closure to questions, problems, and issues; they tend to embrace possibilities—possibilities for changing minds, changing conditions, even changing "truths." Master teachers tend to think in integrated ways.

In the quest for authentic school reform, therefore, we believe that seductive teachers must be creators of Quality Events that bring together curricular reformers and policy/funding/administrative reformers. Seductive teachers know that school reform (synthesis) can result only from the thesis and antithesis of curricular reformers and policy/funding/administrative reformers. For school reform to occur, these two forces must stop competing and become integrated. In other words, they must become whole. There is nothing mystical about this; it is an entirely practical matter.

Seductive teachers become the catalysts for achieving wholeness, the Quality we all covet. To do so requires *gumption*, another of Robert Pirsig's terms. "Gumption," he declares, "is the psychic gasoline that keeps the whole thing going. If you haven't got it there's no way the motorcycle can possibly be fixed" (273). He also speaks of "gumption traps," naming two kinds. One is ". . . those in which you're thrown off the Quality track by conditions that arise from external circumstances" (275). For seductive teachers, these gumption traps might be policy/funding/administrative reforms (more standardized tests, a "national curriculum," students separated in class by gender, "competency guarantees" for graduates, and so on) imposed from without—"reforms" they had no voice in deciding and, therefore, no stake in defending. The other is ". . . traps in which you're thrown off the Quality track by conditions . . . within yourself" (275)—such as an inadvertent return to one of the dualities, a classic or a romantic stance. Master teachers try to dodge such traps to keep on keeping on.

There are many teachers in schools who share the views of curriculum we have described, who understand the importance of building partnerships and relationships with students and colleagues, who integrate subjective and objective views of teaching (characterized by both freedom and discipline), and who maintain gumption. We'll offer just one example. Valerie Klauss is a sixteen-year English teacher at Great Bridge Middle School North in Chesapeake, Virginia. Her principal, Rick West, says about her, "The true test of a principal's confidence in a teacher is that he is willing to entrust his own child's education to her, as I have done with

Valerie Klauss. Valerie has the ability to make all children feel important and valuable while she gets the most possible out of each of them." Klauss's colleague and team partner, William Van Bennekum, says, "Valerie is a dynamic teacher who understands both the emotional and intellectual development of children. The kids know she cares about them and respects them, but she has a presence in the classroom, too. They know she's demanding." One of Valerie Klauss's students. Tamara Cain, observed, "Ms. Klauss *helps* us learn. She's enthusiastic. A lot of the time, it doesn't even seem like work." One of us conducted the following interview with Klauss:

J.A.: How would you define "curriculum"?

V.K.: Well—it's the material we have to teach, but I have the freedom to do the job as I like. My curriculum is English. What's the point of English? It's communication. I try to model good communication with everybody, in and out of the classroom. My kids are as much of the curriculum as anything else. The English curriculum is everything and everybody. I know of too many teachers who don't seem to realize that they have live children in their classrooms. They are too consumed with "curriculum coverage" and administrative approval. The danger of this is that they lose sight of what we're here to do—reach kids. Of course, everyone needs to be satisfied—parents, administrators, yourself—but it's possible, it's possible.

J.A.: What do you do when you detect that something's not working in a particular lesson?

V.K.: I back up and regroup. If I'm teaching a lesson and it's obvious to me that students aren't picking up on whatever the material is, I've got to figure out what went wrong and why they're not getting it. I think flexibility is important. A teacher can't always be sure how her class is receiving what she is teaching, what she is talking about or showing.

J.A.: What are some factors or reasons you've discovered in teaching that cause students not to "get it"?

V.K.: Well, it could be environmental—something as simple as the classroom not being right—or at times, it could be emotional. They might be experiencing a disturbance in the classroom. I can sense when something's wrong, usually. It could be a disagreement between two students or something more powerful happening at home. If you know your students, you know something is not the way it should be, and so what I may have to do is something quite different from what I had planned, something not written in my plan book. I might start by asking students about what's going on. How can you teach the content when you don't know what's going on with your kids? You can't, really. I mean, I suppose I could present the material for that day, but I wouldn't begin to know what they're going to do with it in their heads if I'm not tuned into them, at least to some degree.

J.A.: How are you able to engage students actively in your classroom?

V.K.: Well, I guess it sometimes is a form of trickery. It's like in a writing assignment, students will ask, "How many sentences do we have to write?" I don't answer those kinds of questions. The reason I'm so adamant about that is that all their lives someone has been making decisions for them. I don't want to support that. So I may say, "You decide that. Just do what you think it takes, and we'll see what you come up with. Use your own judgment." Students come to me with preconceived notions, especially about literature. They've read stories and answered questions, read stories and answered questions, on and on. That has to get boring, so I like to do all sorts of things to turn them on to a story. I get *them* to ask the questions, and to assume roles of characters occasionally. Sometimes they want to know more than I'm willing to tell them. It's like holding a carrot. I have to vary the routine of the classroom every day, although there's an underlying structure to what I do that may not be evident to someone observing.

J.A.: How can teachers connect better with their students?

V.K.: We have to look beyond the faces that are looking at us. We have to try to look into their heads *and* their hearts. If we could do that, we could reach in and find what works. It's a matter of finding those avenues of communication. It takes a lot out of you, and it's exhausting. Some teachers aren't willing to do it, but some can be helped to do it better.

J.A.: How can you help other teachers do that?

V.K.: I really enjoy working with other teachers, especially new ones. Often they come in with the idea that you go into the classroom like a lion, that you shouldn't be "nice" to your class. It doesn't have to be that way. There's something fundamentally missing in that belief—respect. My kids know the minute they walk into my room that I will show them respect. I'll give them the space they need, as long as it's real and reasonable. As a result of that, everything falls into place. I think many teachers came, and still come, into the profession thinking kids must just respect them. It doesn't work that way. You don't just get respect, you have to give it. It's true for kids, and it's true for the people you work with, too. You tend to get what you give to others, not all of the time, but a lot of the time.

J.A.: Say more about that, about how you try to work with other teachers.

V.K.: Teachers who model their beliefs have a better chance of effecting change within other teachers. You can't just tell other teachers they're all wet, even if you believe it. Offering help when asked, or lesson ideas, or sharing experiences can work. Good teachers, I think, have to accept opportunities for leadership roles in the school when they come up, too, although it sometimes feels like just a lot of extra work. I've accepted a position next year as a team leader. I'll be working with two relatively new teachers who are a little apprehensive about teaching, and I know they'll be looking for help.

J.A.: Parents and everybody today want their children to receive a "quality education." Everybody wants quality. What do you do to ensure "quality" in your classroom and in your teaching?

V.K.: Well, I'm not sure, but here's what I think. You usually get quality when you give it. I believe it's almost that simple. When students feel important and feel connected to what is happening in the classroom, they respond with quality, the best they can give at the time, whatever that means. I truly believe students will go as far as we can stimulate them to go. We have to help them find their wings, as romantic as that sounds. They need wings to give them the power to go ahead and the discipline it takes to do it.

Seductive teachers maintain gumption, and they know Quality (*wholeness*) when they get it and when they give it; they recognize the need for both freedom and discipline; they resist what they believe opposes Quality; and they promote harmony, the enabling agent of Quality. Nothing short of Quality—as we have considered it here and as this interview suggests—will bring about genuinely helpful school reform.

References

Glasser, William. 1990. *The Quality School.* New York, NY: Harper Perennial.

Pirsig, Robert. 1974. *Zen and the Art of Motorcycle Maintenance.* New York, NY: Bantam Books.

Chapter Five

Schooling for Self-Efficacy
Environment Building

The current habit of dualistic thinking sets up road-blocks to school reform that inhibit it from working on what truly counts—teaching and learning. We're arguing for a synthesis of curricular reform and policy/funding/administrative reform to set school improvement efforts on a Quality track. Either/or thinking creates situations in which these two basic approaches collide and compete with each other. Until they become integrated (whole), current school reform movements will remain stuck in their own inertia, like other such movements of the past.

Another place where school reform movements are off the Quality track is in the current controversy over self-esteem, silly though the issue seems. There are those who believe that a sense of high self-esteem is a necessary precondition for achieving anything; there are others who believe that achievement is a necessary precondition for acquiring self-esteem. It's the chicken-or-egg question: which comes first?

It appears that any school reform effort claiming to be student-centered raises a red flag to those who assume that academic achievement precedes self-esteem. This preference for academics (object) over self-esteem (subject) is yet another example of classic-oriented thinking. So-called outcome-based education is a case in point. It's a strategy for school reform that a number of states adopted in the 1980s and then abandoned in the 1990s, because of criticism from classic-oriented thinkers. The Minnesota State Department of Education describes it this way.

> Education that is outcome-based is a learner-centered, results-
> oriented system founded on the belief that all individuals can
> learn. In this system: 1) What is to be learned is clearly identi-
> fied; 2) Learners' progress is based on demonstrated achieve-
> ment; 3) Multiple instructional and assessment strategies are
> available to meet the needs of each learner; 4) Time and assis-
> tance are provided for each learner to reach maximum potential.
> (Towers 1994, 625)

Outcome-based education, as well as other reform efforts that smack of learner-centeredness (as referred to in the Minnesota statement), is suspect to classic thinkers. The focus on learners (who) rather than on the content and processes (what) of a curriculum seems wrong to them. Their criticism centers on how such an approach coddles youngsters instead of challenges them. A kind of sloganis-tic refrain has emerged in the classic camp of school critics against student-centered reform. It goes something like this, "They aren't going to *learn* anything, but they're sure going to *feel* good about it!" As Robert L. Simonds, president of the National Association of Christian Educators and Citizens for Excellence in Education, has expressed it, "When you add up all the time devoted to . . . 'self es-teem'. . . where is time found to teach the academics needed for a successful life?" (1994, 13).

A report in the *Virginian-Pilot* newspaper on May 25, 1994, be-gan this way, "Vowing to turn schools' attention away from molding student attitudes and self-esteem, Governor George F. Allen on Tuesday announced a 49-member commission charged with draft-ing a plan for education reform in Virginia" (B3). (No public school teachers are mentioned in the article as members of the commis-sion, although one elementary school principal's name appears.) A little over three months later, on September 2, 1994, another article in the same newspaper, reported by Vanee Vines, announced the following policy/funding/administrative proposals from the forty-nine member panel, "Longer school days and school years. Student uniforms. Tuition tax credits . . . Single gender classes . . . 'compe-tency guarantees' for graduates" (B3). The either/or thinking trap strikes again, not only in Virginia but also in many other places.

Those who believe in learner-centered schools, on the other hand, take a different view. They believe that teachers must first work on enhancing students' self-esteem before anything else. They pay attention to media reports of school violence, the literacy prob-lem, and other such depressing news; their "hearts go out" to stu-dents facing immense psychosocial problems today. Professor Nel Noddings of Stanford University laments "the deadly notion that the schools' first priority should be intellectual development" (1992, 12); she prefers instead that "the main aim of education should be to produce competent, caring, loving, and lovable people" (174).

Parents, also, lament the presence of increasingly hostile, unmotivated students in classrooms. They fear for the safety of their children and their children's teachers in the company of students whose behavior is often violent and resistant to everything that school seems to stand for. Learner-centered teachers who lean sharply to the romantic side want to "save" every student. All they need to do, they believe, is make students feel better about who they are and where they come from; then they will succeed. "If only students cared more about themselves," our romantic-oriented colleagues reason, "they wouldn't do harmful things, harmful to themselves and others."

Again, dualistic thinking hinders genuine progress. Arguably, for a long time Adolph Hitler appeared to feel pretty good about himself and about his Aryan race in general, but that fact alone didn't stop him from wreaking major havoc in Europe. So, is self-esteem enough? Is academic achievement enough? Which comes first?

Let us pause long enough to be clear about our intention here. We do not mean to endorse nor to condemn the outcome-based education movement nor any other specific one; neither do we mean to endorse or to condemn *critics* of one reform movement or another. Our aim is to show that one-way thinking tends to lead down a path to nowhere. If we wish to find the "truth," we must think in integrated ways, ways that bring schools and communities together rather than divide them into distinct camps. The self-esteem controversy is an enemy to genuine school reform because it fortifies the barriers that exist between curricular reformers and policy/funding/administrative reformers.

Yet, we do have a controversy to contend with, so let's pursue it further. First, according to education critic Alfie Kohn, no empirical research seems to support either position that high self-esteem necessarily produces achievement or that achievement necessarily produces high self-esteem (1994, 280). School is, or ought to be, however, about meeting students' needs; therefore, it seems reasonable to ask, "What do human beings need?" In his landmark article of more than fifty years ago, "A Theory of Human Motivation," Abraham Maslow, distinguished psychologist and learning theorist, identified what he called a "hierarchy of needs." There are five in his well-known scheme: biological requirements (sleep, food), safety, affiliation with others, self-esteem, and self-actualization (the need to become all that one is capable of becoming) (1943, 370–396). Other psychologists, like Edward Decci and Richard Ryan of the University of Rochester, have identified three fundamental needs: to be autonomous, to be competent, and to be related to others (1990, 243). Like Maslow, William Glasser also identifies five human needs: survival, love, power, fun, and freedom (1990, 43). Glasser argues that everything a school does should aim toward satisfying one or more of these basic human needs, while everything else should be scrapped.

This way of thinking reminds us of Neil Postman's call, nearly two decades ago, for a "thermostatic" view of education (1979, 19–20). What he meant was that schools should work at doing only those things for students that the society doesn't already do for them: for example, if the larger society teaches students to *compete*, the school curriculum should focus on teaching them to *cooperate*.

Looked at within the context of human needs, would anybody in his or her right mind seriously argue against the quest for self-esteem? Maslow includes it directly in his famous hierarchy, and Decci and Ryan and Glasser implicitly embrace it. (How, for instance, can one love, seek power, have fun, and achieve freedom in healthy ways without possessing or acquiring a pretty high sense of self-esteem along the way?) Furthermore, if Postman's perspective has merit, schools should be working to help students *raise* their self-esteem, especially when elements within the larger society (including many students' families and peers) often serve to *lower* it. It seems reasonable that attention to self-esteem belongs in the curriculum. We all want it and need it. It's how and where we get it that's really at issue. For many students, school may be the most likely place.

So, does a sense of high self-esteem precede achievement, or is it the other way around? Our answer is yes. Achievement can cause one's self-esteem to rise, and high self-esteem can help one to achieve (that is to say, a healthy sense of self-esteem never hurts). The phenomenon is more circular than linear. It must be true that school achievement and self-esteem go hand in glove; they are mutually dependent; they are *one*, not two separate things. It's not a question of either/or; it's a question of both/and—integration (wholeness). Any school improvement effort that values one over the other misses the point and handicaps itself mightily.

Schools cannot afford to ignore the importance of high self-esteem in a student's pursuit of academic success; neither can they afford to ignore the importance of academic success while working to raise students' self-esteem. So we're looking at something of a paradox—a lock without a key, a canoe without a paddle. It is neither sensible nor viable to go for one without the other. Achievement and self-esteem are like that—twin sides of a single coin.

Good teachers do not become paralyzed over issues like the self-esteem controversy. They know that it's a conundrum, a bit of a silly riddle—like how many angels can sit on the head of a pin, perhaps fun to muse about but not very productive if you're seriously interested in reaching and teaching students. What good teachers are after is a synthesis of self-esteem and achievement. We might call that synthesis self-efficacy, the power one feels to produce effects—to learn, to succeed, to do better, to keep trying, to grow. The best teachers know that self-efficacy results from the thesis and antithesis, if you will, of self-esteem and achievement. (We know and you know that self-esteem and achievement are not opposites, but some school reform rhetoric suggests otherwise.)

In good teachers' classrooms, then, we do not see a preference for the humanistic (romantic) tradition over the scientific (classic) tradition. We do not see a preference for valuing self-esteem over academic excellence. What we do see is teachers acting on their knowledge that the curriculum is both a *who* and a *what*. The *who* is the learner, and the *what* is the stuff to be learned. Students who do well in school tend to have a high degree of self-efficacy already; so, excellent teachers spend little time building such students' self-esteem, because there is little, if any, need to do so. Other students, however, do not do so well; where school is concerned, they do not have a highly developed sense of self-efficacy. Good teachers know the importance of spending time with these students, in and out of class, to help them see that they *can* break their patterns of failure and begin to succeed. That takes a special effort, which good teachers habitually give.

Stating the case a little differently, Professor Thomas Lasley puts it,

> Every class and school includes some trouble-makers and some nobodies. The attention teachers pay (or don't pay) to these students has short- and long-term negative effects. Simply acknowledging the presence of these students can make a big difference. . . . The self-images of all students derive from the types of interactions they have with adults. And these self-images form the foundation of their subsequent failure or success. . . . (1987, 677)

Here are two examples of how excellent teachers pay attention to students, to both their feeling lives and their academic lives. Gary Cohagan is a teacher in Clovis, California. Writing about his work, Sonia Nazario reports in a special feature on education in *The Wall Street Journal*,

> ... when [Mr. Cohagan] exhibits caring, by regularly attending
> his students' sporting games or calling them on weekends ...,
> they respond with trust. ... [One student] who couldn't read
> learned perseverance when Mr. Cohagan repeatedly stayed after
> school to read the sports pages with him. By the end of the year,
> [the student] was one of the class's best readers. (1992, 3)

Good teachers know that students are not robots but feeling, thinking human beings, and such teachers act accordingly. Giving time to students in the ways Gary Cohagan does is often just the catalyst students need to become successful. Both achievement and self-esteem tend to rise when students see that teachers value them as human beings, not just "clients."

Yet another example is 1994 National Teacher of the Year Sandra McBrayer. In *The Virginian-Pilot* on September 22, 1994, reporter Jon Glass quotes her saying, "I don't just teach math, science, and history. I teach life—how to communicate with one another, how to end a conflict in a peaceful manner, how to get what you need without taking it" (B3). Life is not merely physical, nor merely intellectual; it's also emotional. How learners feel matters, as seductive teachers everywhere know. Teaching is largely a matter of working on the problem of *motivation*, and motivation comes from the deepest recesses within both the mind and the heart.

Professors David L. Clark and Terry A. Astuto have noted, "True motivators are linked to *personal growth and achievement*"; they add that the large bulk of research on motivation" ... demonstrates the importance of a student's assuming responsibility for learning and building a sense of *efficacy* as a learner" (1994, 515). Seductive teachers' knowledge is often far ahead of educational research conducted by "outsiders." Seductive teachers measure their success in terms of how far their students move from a point of dependence to a point of independence over the course of a school year. They know that, while test scores and other quantitative measures of achievement are important to the media and the general public, this qualitative measure of movement from a state of dependence to one of independence is more important to the schooling process itself.

Bill Etzel, a teacher we know at Bellport Middle School in Bellport, New York, illustrates our point. In his classroom are a number of students who are not particularly adept with Standard English. In fact, his is a school in which many students measure respect by behavior and reputation on the street more than in the classroom. Etzel reaches his students by asking them to wade in shallow water before expecting them to swim in the deep. In one lesson on the Civil War, he shows his students slides that he took at Harpers

Ferry, and he begins a discussion about John Brown's famous raid on the Federal arsenal there. One student sees from the slides that an arsenal looks like some sort of fortified building—really a house. He asks Mr. Etzel what the word *arsenal* means.

For some teachers, in the midst of a history lesson/lecture, the options for answering a question like "What's an arsenal?" are limited. One could provide a dictionary definition, give a modified definition in the teacher's own words, request that another student answer, or suggest that students look up the word "on your own time" The goal is to keep on track, on schedule, within the lesson plan. Slowing the pace of instruction to deal with a simple question seems a nuisance. Seductive teachers often take a different tack. They see such questions as "What's an arsenal?" as an opportunity to make the lesson plan work better rather than as an interruption to deal with quickly and then move on.

Etzel remembers that a few of his students play on the community soccer teams and that they have spoken to him about British soccer teams they watch on television. He recalls that one of these teams is the Arsenal. He asks Katie, "Do you remember that English soccer team you told me about—the one with the unusual name and the red jerseys you liked? What was it?" Katie replies, "Oh, you mean the Arsenal?" Mr. Etzel says, "Yeah, that's the one. Why do you think they call the team that?" Katie responds, "I guess because they have one of the best teams." Mr. Etzel says, "I bet you're right. Are they that good? Would you imagine that a lot of their players might be a threat to score at any time? Do you think they have a lot of weapons to use against other teams?" Katie adds, "Well they score a lot when I watch 'em, and their nickname is the Gunners." Mr. Etzel now turns to the whole class, "Hey, did any of you watch the US team in the Olympics? They had players who could shoot like cannons! I heard the announcer say that one player could bang the ball about seventy-five miles an hour and that the whole team had a lot of weapons they could use to score with. Does anybody see any connection between all this and the word *arsenal?*" A lot of hands go up and a flurry of commotion erupts. Bill Etzel smiles. He has taught a vocabulary lesson that all students "got" today.

He returns to his slides on John Brown and the raid on Harpers Ferry. One hand is still up. "Yeah, Antonio? What?" Antonio says, "Hey man, I got some soccer cards with them Arsenal players, you know?" Antonio never says much; this is the first time in a long while. Bill Etzel smiles again. "Well, bring 'em in. You can show them to the class. I'd like to see these guys who think they're such powerful weapons." The class is amused, but Antonio has an "assignment."

Some might consider what happened in this class as merely a trivial aside, certainly not a significant moment in a serious history lesson. Seductive teachers, however, know that such occurrences can make all the difference in the success of a lesson, that such moments have far-reaching impact on students and their willingness to learn other things. Bill Etzel's students were allowed to use their experience and to take some ownership of language.

When students—all students—enter a classroom at the beginning of the year, they must at first depend on the teacher. To have a chance at success, they need to know what they will be studying and learning, what the teachers' expectations are, how they will be evaluated, how they will be working together in the classroom, and so on. Over time, good teachers win students' trust. They give students increasingly more rope—not for hanging themselves but for taking charge of their learning (an important distinction). Seductive teachers give students increasingly more authority to make their own decisions, define and solve their own problems, ask and answer their own questions, and to assume more responsibility in general for making the classroom community "work." The best teachers know they have failed if students remain dependent upon them throughout the year; they know they've succeeded when they see students developing self-efficacy.

A sign of trouble, over time, is the persistence of questions like, "How long does this paper have to be? What am I supposed to do now (or next)? Did you do anything yesterday when I wasn't here? (Of course not, Antonio, we wouldn't do anything when you weren't here!) How do you want this done? Are you counting off for spelling? Why don't you just tell us the answer? Are you going to tell us what's going to be on the test? Can I borrow a pencil and some paper? Why do we have to do this stuff, anyway? Do we have to take notes?" Questions like these signal teachers that something is wrong. They know it's time to take stock—to pause for what coaches call "skull sessions." It's time to discuss what the classroom is about (yet again), what the mission is, why things aren't moving forward, what everybody needs to do to succeed, and that everybody can succeed. Occasional sessions like this take time away from "covering material," but only if you think the curriculum is a what and not also a who. When students lose confidence, lose sight of their goals and purposes, lose their "center" as learners, they also lose ground in the struggle to achieve independence. And they lose their sense of self-efficacy. They are thrown off the Quality track.

Seductive teachers know that progress toward helping students develop self-efficacy as learners is never smooth, sure, and straight. It's nearly always rough, jerky, and winding. As in a garden, the classroom territory has to be tilled more than once, the seeds sometimes replanted, and the buds nourished and attended to regularly. It's the same for all living things. But the journey teachers and students undertake in classrooms, with and without a map, must be an engaging one. When it is, students feel good about themselves and about being there. It comes down to this: *learning depends upon willingness, engagement, and a desire for more autonomy*. When these factors are alive in learners, so are self-esteem and the drive to succeed.

A willingness to learn and an engagement in learning have much to do with how students feel about themselves, certainly, but also about their schools, their classrooms, and their teachers. The better they feel about *all* these, the more they are likely to achieve; and the more they achieve, the better they are likely to feel. It all adds up in the end to independence, i.e., a state of being in control, of being able to think, feel, and do for oneself. It adds up to a sense of "wholeness," and that is what good teachers are after.

The "down-side" of teachers' relentless attention to the whole lives of students, of course, is the ever present threat of burnout. This is a condition that occurs when one is led to say, "I can't do it anymore," or "I can't take it anymore." It's the nemesis of every workaholic. (Of course, you can't burn out if you've never been on fire.) Burnout is a real issue, however, and we do not intend to dismiss it whimsically. Any teacher can experience burnout, but teachers who truly involve themselves with students are perhaps at greatest risk.

Teachers who encounter students in many settings—classrooms, extra-class activities, and elsewhere—often find, when they do a little addition, that they're spending fifty-plus hours per week (perhaps some weekends, as well) in the company of students and/or colleagues. Even if they enjoy all that time—as good teachers tend to do—they (not to mention their significant others) still have a sense that they're always working. They notice that they're staying after school long after many other teachers have gone home, and they secretly wonder, "Who's smarter, me or the ones who left?" The romantic-oriented teachers, because of their intense interest in and association with students (as well as their determination to "save" them all) are candidates for quick burnout; the classic-oriented teachers, because of their frustration over the "problem of student apathy" (as they might phrase it), are just as liable to succumb, if not as quickly.

Seductive teachers, on the other hand, work to achieve whole-ness in their perspectives and in their lives in general, both at work and at play. Unlike the romantic teachers, they know they cannot "save" all students, although they try very hard to do so. (Jesus chose twelve disciples but got one lemon, and teachers don't even get to select who comes to their classrooms.) Unlike classic-orient-ed teachers, seductive ones know they *can* do something about stu-dent apathy. They tend to find many avenues for renewing and rewarding themselves. They love their profession, but they enjoy other aspects of their lives, as well, and they are more often than not successful in balancing the facets of their existence. We're not sug-gesting they never burn out; they might. But it's usually a slow burn, seldom a conflagration. Seductive teachers, in other words, tend to maintain a high sense of self-efficacy and "wholeness" themselves, and they model it for their students and colleagues.

Seductive teachers are successful because they value and mod-el the attitudinal traits and behaviors they wish their students and colleagues to acquire and develop: balance, harmony, and whole-ness in life. A significant feature of this balance, harmony, and wholeness is a recognition of the mutual dependency of self-esteem and achievement. If school reform is to take hold, it, too, must rec-ognize this mutual dependency. The school reform movement must enlist and enable the best teachers to show others the importance of integrating attention to students' self-esteem *and* achievement. Thinking and behaving in integrated ways can move us forward; desperately holding on to singular perspectives can keep us stuck.

School reform efforts, in many places, have become polarized and stalled by the self-esteem controversy. It is an issue that ob-structs progress. School reformers must stop bickering over "how many angels can sit on the head of a pin." They must look to seduc-tive teachers for help in achieving the integrated effort toward school reform that will make a positive difference in the lives of youngsters. Anything less is just politics, the appearance of reform without its necessary substance. So what kind of school achieves an integration of self-esteem and achievement?

Students and teachers must perceive their classrooms as safe places where they feel free to make mistakes because mistakes pre-cede growth. Both students and teachers must see their classrooms as welcoming, hospitable places if they are to look forward to com-ing to school each day. They must possess a sense of mutual owner-ship of schools if they are to feel they have a stake in what happens there. They must see their schools as places where everybody is re-sponsible for everyone else's learning. Through such perceptions and feelings as these, students and teachers acquire a sense of community, a sense that "we're all in this together, and we're all responsible for making things work in this place in this time." This kind of "environment-building" is what makes schools work for everyone.

What happens when students and teachers *don't* see their schools in these ways? In Eric Lax's biography *Woody*, actor/director Woody Allen describes going to school, "It was an odious task. You'd leave your house on a cold, wet winter morning despising having . . . to leave the comforts of your little bed and your radio and the things that were so wonderful. And you'd go to the school, where all was hostility and problems . . .". He recalls his school as "the dread place" that he "hated more than rat poison" and standing on line in the mornings waiting to go to that "abysmal horror" that was school (1991, 31). Regardless of how you (or we) think that Woody Allen turned out, he paints a rather clear and severe picture of his vision of school. Unfortunately, of course, his attitudes are by no means unique. They are shared by all too many students in generations that succeeded him. Ultimately, it is the teacher's vision that creates a classroom learning environment, and students can see it as inviting, challenging, and warm, or they can see it as repelling, chilling, and dull. English teachers who decide to lead can help both students and colleagues see it as inviting, challenging, and warm.

Let us be quick to add that the image of school Woody Allen provides is certainly not peculiar to the twentieth century. It is not time-bound. There are few, if any, basics to go back to here. Charles Dickens describes a stark and austere classroom of more than a hundred years ago, a classroom ruled by the schoolmaster Mr. Thomas Gradgrind. Dickens writes, "The scene was a plain, bare monotonous vault of a school room, and . . . the emphasis was helped by the speaker's voice, which was inflexible, dry and dictatorial." Gradgrind sees his students as "little pitchers before him, who were to be filled so full of facts" (1854, 5). In one scene, Mr. Gradgrind calls upon a girl to recite the dictionary definition of a horse. She begins by revealing that her father trains horses. Gradgrind quickly stops this tangential response by pointing his finger and bellowing, "Girl number 20. We don't want to know anything about that here. You mustn't tell us about that here." Concerned only with a student's ability to retain and recite "accurate" textbook "facts," Gradgrind announces to the class, "Girl number 20 unable to define a horse! Girl number 20 possessed of no facts in reference to one of the commonest animals!" (5–6).

Gradgrind-like exercises still exist in school, of course. You might recall them yourself. You may have been asked to stand before your classmates and teachers to recite, say, the periodic table of the elements in eleventh-grade chemistry. Your voice was perhaps expressionless, flat, and monotonous as you struggled to recall, and your classmates "listened" either with polite indifference or with outright disdain made manifest by distorted faces and unkind "humor." (Classmates who had survived their own turns at the task seemed to take pleasure in your torture. Knowing the periodic table of the elements may have been worthwhile—we're not suggesting it wasn't—but the chart seemed to be the focus of the learning you were to do, with no larger purpose that you could discern at the moment. Familiar? (We hope not.)

Seductive teachers know that classroom environments do not have to resemble Gradgrind's—in fact, must not. Instead of defining a classroom by competition, seductive teachers opt for cooperation; instead of defining it by individual isolation, seductive teachers opt for community; instead of defining it strictly by the teacher's judgment, seductive teachers opt for help, help from everyone in the room toward the end of defining and measuring success for all.

What we are discussing here is the *abstract* classroom environment, because that's the one we believe is supremely important. The other kind is *physical*—that is, what you can literally see and touch, such as teachers' and students' desks and their placements, size and configuration of space, wall composition and color, instructional material and equipment (ideally, the most up-to-date technology available), floors, (preferably with carpet), blinds or curtains on windows (if there are windows), and furniture and furnishings other than desks. These things are important, too, just not as important. If you disagree, at least hear us out for a moment.

Some school reform efforts suggest that the physical environment may be more important than nearly anything else. Incredible amounts of money are spent each year on school buildings, erecting and renovating them. We believe, as we have said before, that far more resources should be used to attract, increase, and keep seductive teachers than to do anything else, as helpful as other things might be. Seductive teachers, in greater numbers, must be the top priority; everything else is secondary to that crucial need. Buildings and technology are important, but people are even *more* important. Teachers, after all, must create the abstract learning environment that is more influential on student learning than is the physical environment. What matters most is that teachers and students perceive their meeting place, whatever its physical appearance and character, as their turf, a place where they come to be and work together. That is what makes a profound difference between reform that works and reform that doesn't.

John Slade, a seductive teacher presently working in Norway, writes in "Letters from an American Teacher in Russia" about his high school classroom in St. Petersburg,

> My Russian students wear sweaters and scarves in a chilly room built nearly three centuries ago. The windows facing the frozen river are taped shut; the air, laden with cigarette smoke and chalk dust, is months old. . . . schools with few books and severely limited supplies, doing a superb job. (1994, 15)

Seductive teachers are never obsolete anywhere in the world. Physical facilities, equipment, and instructional materials—to the seductive teacher—are like brushes and pallets in an artist's hands. Necessary, certainly, but without the teacher (artist), they are useless. Policymakers and decision makers who fund schools must understand, ultimately, that the heart of a school—its overall spirit—does not depend entirely upon the school's physical structure, the size of the cafeteria, the seating capacity of the stadium or gym, the acoustics of the auditorium, furnishings in offices and lounges, or any other inanimate objects. What counts is seductive teachers—far more of them than currently exist—practicing their craft.

Few teachers, seductive or otherwise, would turn down opportunities to work within state-of-the-art school buildings and classrooms or with state-of-the-art instructional equipment and materials. It turns out, though, that state-of-the-art anything (buildings, textbooks, technology, and so on) is generally worthless without armies of seductive teachers managing and handling it. Funding through school reform, therefore, must consider that principle for truly improving students' achievement.

Here's an analogy to underscore what we are getting at. A young girl visits a doctor's office to get a shot for the flu. The physical character of the office is pleasant and inviting; the overstuffed leather chairs, comfortable; the piped-in music, soothing. The subdued accent of thick fabric curtains, the flocked wallpaper, and the plush carpet are all intended to produce a calming effect. Lurking beneath this surface, however, lives the "real problem." No matter how she tries to avoid the inevitable reality, the girl knows what awaits in the doctor's examining room. Only a few steps away is a place that will snap her out of her false sense of security and comfort. She's going to get a shot! There are no two ways about it, and it's going to hurt. She will not accept the notion that "It's going to be good for you."

The cough suddenly seems less bothersome, the fever less intense, the pain more tolerable. She wants out of this place! The smell assaults her; the stainless steel blinds her; fear overwhelms her. The immediacy of the moment (mixed with apprehension on the verge of terror) and the expectation of shock counteract the positive effects of any sedate decor or soft music. This experience is going to be painful, no matter how you cut it.

Now what ultimately will happen to this girl depends not on the physical surroundings of the doctor's office, but on the doctor. If the doctor is a seductive one, the girl will come back again and again, realizing "it wasn't so bad" as she thought. If not, she may never come back. So it is in a classroom, regardless of physical trappings.

Seductive teaching begins with the creation of an enriched learning environment—the inner, intangible space of schools and classroom. This space must not only allow but breed among students a sense of safety, hospitality, freedom, responsibility, and caring about learning together. Such a sense is contagious. If these qualities are present, students stand to learn the "stuff" of the paper curriculum. Not incidentally, also, they will learn to respect and to appreciate the adults around them, as well as each other.

In *The Dragons of Eden*, Carl Sagan cites evidence of the impact of environment on learning. He reports,

> [Two researchers at UC-Berkeley] . . . maintained two different
> populations of laboratory rats, one in a dull, repetitive . . .
> environment; the other in a variegated, lively, enriched environment. The latter group displayed a striking increase in the mass
> and thickness of the cerebral cortex. . . . Since a more massive
> cerebral cortex may make future learning easier, the importance of
> enriched . . . environments . . . is clearly drawn. (45)

Granted, human beings aren't rats. They are smarter and more sensitive, with more highly developed cerebral cortices. They stand to benefit even more than rats from "variegated, lively, enriched environments." Such environments have both a physical and an abstract character, and each is important. Clearly, there are school buildings in the United States that are rat- and pigeon-infested, that have peeling lead paint, that stink, and that are in other ways appalling. Such physical environments need immediate attention, of course. We abhor, along with you, the appalling physical conditions of some school structures in the United States today. In a *Virginian-Pilot* editorial on July 24, 1996, a State Department of Education report was cited, "52 percent of Virginia schools have deferred maintenance needs; 43 percent are using temporary classrooms; 30 percent of classrooms are overcrowded; 27 percent of facilities are obsolete; 32

percent need air conditioning; 20 percent have problems with contaminants like asbestos or leaded paint" (A14). All of this in a state that is largely rural—never mind places like New York City, Chicago, or Los Angeles. Still, seductive teachers do their best to create healthy abstract learning environments, and students grow in them—physically, emotionally, and intellectually. For human beings, physical environments are important, but intangible ones—characterized by mutually respectful human relationships—are even more crucial, *especially* in dire physical settings.

As we have argued, the criteria that define a seductive learning environment go way beyond the physical. What are some of these criteria? We list five and comment on each one separately. They are essential for creating healthy classrooms and healthy schools, in which teachers work together to help one another grow.

1. Learning environments must be challenging, involving authentic problems and issues that demand students to inquire into them and to decide about them.

2. Learning environments must involve communal activity—teachers and students working cooperatively to share their experience and knowledge for the good of the group.

3. Learning environments must require students to examine problems, questions, and issues from a variety of perspectives.

4. Learning environments must encourage and allow students to monitor their own learning—that is, think, talk, and write (reflect) about what they're doing and how they're doing it.

5. Learning environments must be action-oriented, with students behaving as workers and teachers as leaders who can attract students and win them over to valuing their learning tasks.

First, *learning environments must be challenging, involving authentic problems and issues that demand students to inquire into them and to decide about them.* When students spend most of their time on tasks that come easy, what they learn is that tasks come easy. When they spend most of their time, however, on tasks that are challenging, what they learn is that tasks are challenging. To learn how to inquire, students must inquire; to learn how to make decisions, students must make decisions. To see the connections between academic work in school and their lives outside of school, they must engage in academic work that is grounded in authentic (real world) contexts. Mere exercises won't get the job done. A. H. Schoenfeld, as reported in Marcy Driscoll's book *Psychology of Learning for Instruction*, offers an example of how students are able to perform mathematical operations—that is, get the numerical answer right—without understanding the relevance or purpose of the actual problem (1994, 159–160). A group of thirteen-year-olds were given this word problem to solve. An army bus holds thirty-six soldiers. If 1,128 soldiers are being bused to their training site, how many buses are needed? Seventy percent of the group showed that they knew how to solve the mathematical part of the problem—divide 1,128 by thirty-six to get an answer of thirty-one with a remainder of twelve. But only twenty-three percent of the group gave the right answer within the context of the problem: how many buses are needed? (The answer, of course, is 32 buses.) Chances are that the majority of these students never learned what mathematics is for—to solve authentic problems. When students merely practice "skills"—such as long division—isolated from any genuine use or context, they have difficulty when someone asks them to use the skills in solving an actual problem. The issue is not about how many times thirty-six goes into 1,128; it's about how many buses are needed by the soldiers, an actual problem that mathematics as a tool can solve, but as a means rather than an end.

Connecting the teaching of skills to authentic problems and issues takes more time than merely doing exercises. But it's better to slow down the pace of instruction to pose and to accommodate genuine problems and issues than it is merely to engage students in skills exercises for their own sake. In other words, seductive teachers know that when they cover less—when they slow down the pace of instruction to make learning real—students tend to uncover more.

Second, *learning environments must involve communal activity— teachers and students working cooperatively to share their experience and knowledge for the good of the group.* To state this criterion more succinctly, we learn from others. Seductive learning environments often require students to teach each other. As we have repeated several times, teaching is a powerful way of learning; therefore, it should not be restricted to teachers alone. Seductive teachers know that they must not do all the "telling" in their classrooms (or in their schools). They must set up situations in which students work collaboratively, in which students tell and teach each other. Students and teachers who work together, sharing what they know and don't know and seeking help from others who can fill in the gaps, learn things for good because those things are won through arduous and fully engaged effort.

Communal learning does not mean that teachers must always require students to work in small groups, although that is important for students to do. It can also mean that in whole class discussions, everyone stands to learn from everyone else. Seductive teachers often remind students that their job in the classroom is to listen actively to everyone who speaks, not just to themselves. Seductive teachers sometimes require students to repeat or paraphrase what a classmate has just said as a condition of being allowed to speak themselves.

When community-centered classrooms are working, seductive teachers rarely have discipline problems because everyone is involved productively with everyone else. As George H. Wood writes in *Schools That Work*,

> Discipline comes from enticing and exciting classroom activity and a genuine commitment to the classroom as a community;" . . . classroom management is not an add-on; rather, everything. . . works to foster the sort of self-discipline necessary to make communal life possible. (1992, 93)

Even if there were better ways of teaching "academics," communal learning environments would still be worthwhile because, for many students, school may be the only place where they have a chance to learn the skills, processes, and values of cooperation. The larger society—the democratic society in which schools are presumably preparing students to live and work—demands citizens who can cooperate as well as compete, maybe cooperate more than compete.

Third, *learning environments must require students to examine problems, questions, and issues from a variety of perspectives.* The old adage about the need to "walk a mile in another person's moccasins" applies here. Teachers and students of history, for example, might look at the account of America's decision to drop the atomic bomb on Hiroshima and Nagasaki in August 1945 from several national perspectives. How might that event be reported in an American history textbook? In a Japanese textbook? In a textbook used by students and teachers in a "neutral" country, such as Finland? Such an exploration or project as this gives students a clearer sense that history is merely a matter of perspective, not just fact—that history is written by people; it wasn't found under a rock or on a stone tablet. Or, an English teacher might ask students to argue an issue from several different points of view as they learn to write persuasive and compelling essays. And so on.

It's also important that students learn how to use all their senses, really use them. What can we learn from one sense that we can't learn from another? Color, for example. We must be able to see a color to discern it fully. Texture. We must be able to touch an object to get a full sense of its composition. Exploring alternatives, trying to see and appreciate another's point of view, developing open-mindedness, considering different angles for attacking a problem—these activities and abilities go a long way toward defining truly educated and self-efficacious individuals. Again, we are talking here about *slowing down the pace of instruction*. Looking at questions, problems, and issues from multiple perspectives requires more time than does looking from a single perspective. Yet, in seductive teachers' classrooms, the learning that accrues from multiple perspectives is well worth the added time and effort.

Fourth, *learning environments must encourage and allow students to monitor their own learning—that is, think, talk, and write about what they're doing and how they're doing it*. In *Barefoot in Athens*, his play about the life and death of Socrates, Maxwell Anderson attributes these lines to the great Greek philosopher, "The unexamined life is not worth living; the unexamined life is built on lies; only a world of slaves can live by lies" (1951, III. 2). The contemplative life enables one to acquire self-knowledge; furthermore, it is essential to the health of a democracy, which is only as strong as its members. Democracy depends upon people who make a habit of questioning, of defining and solving problems, and of making decisions that are good for themselves and others. Schooling in a democracy must promote, enable, and facilitate the development of such habits of mind and behavior.

How can schooling accomplish such a goal, beyond present levels? One answer, often neglected, is to allow students time for reflecting, for thinking back. Seductive teachers know that using time in this way is certainly not a waste. In some teachers' classrooms, everything always seems to be moving forward in a frenzied effort to cover material—a "fact-centered" environment. Seductive teachers' classrooms, on the other hand, are places where "time-outs" occur on a regular basis. During these intervals, seductive teachers may lead discussions about purposes for learning tasks in which students have been engaged, or they may create small groups in which such discussions occur. Seductive teachers know that some of the best teaching they do is in getting students to think about what they're doing, as well as why and how they're doing it. They often ask questions like these, both to individuals and to the class as a whole: "Why are we doing this 'old stuff' anyway? How did you go about solving that problem? Where do you think you went wrong and why? What are some alternative ways of going about this job? What are some advantages and disadvantages of this approach? What do you need around you in order to do your best? At what time of day or night do you think you work best and why? Why do you think you're responding (or behaving) as you are right now?

What do you need to do differently in order to do better? How would you evaluate the effort you are making in this classroom? How can you apply what we've been doing to some practical need you might have? What goals should we set for ourselves this week? What do you think will happen next and why? Why do you think so-and-so did what he or she did? How can you defend your point of view? How can you refute so-and-so's argument? How can you state this matter in your own words? What is your own personal position and why? What pattern do you see emerging here? What examples can you think of for this point? What conditions are necessary for this to occur?" And—last but definitely not least—"HOW YA' DOIN'—I MEAN, PERSONALLY?"

Questions such as these, to which students respond by both talking and writing, force students to monitor their own thinking—to become, literally, students of their own thinking processes and behaviors. In classrooms where students engage in reflection and introspection, they *learn how to learn* and to think for themselves. They grow toward becoming independent, self-efficacious learners.

Fifth, *learning environments must be action-oriented, with students behaving as workers and teachers as leaders who can attract students and win them over to valuing their learning tasks.* As Theodore Sizer, noted school reformer and leader of the Coalition of Essential Schools, writes in the closing lines of *Horace's Compromise*, "Inspiration, hunger: these are the qualities that drive good schools. The best we . . . can do is to create the most likely conditions for them to flourish, and then to get out of [the] way" (1984, 221). Some teachers feel they aren't doing their jobs unless they are always in the center of their classrooms, driving students onward to succeed. In this model, however, the teacher is usually the "teller" and students are the "absorbers," whose job is to listen, read their lessons, and perform "exercises." Seductive teachers realize that their larger (and more difficult) job is to create an atmosphere in their classrooms characterized by inspiration and hunger, because students must possess these qualities if learning is to matter and if it is to last.

Seductive teachers know that they are most likely to help students acquire these essential qualities by insisting that their classrooms be active places in which students are doing work that matters—finding out things for themselves, talking and writing about substantive issues (not just listening, reading, or viewing), and developing an ever-increasing sense of curiosity about the "stuff" of the curriculum. As we have said, this job isn't easy; but, it's the job that counts. Marcy Driscoll writes, "As for the concern that students do not all 'buy into' the notion of managing their own learning...teachers must persuade them" (372). Easy to say, sometimes not so easy to do. Yet, it is this ability to "persuade them" that clearly defines the seductive teacher—the teacher who leads, attracts, and wins over students to valuing their learning, and, therefore, valuing themselves.

We are led, then, to a final observation about schooling for self-efficacy through classroom environment building, a kind of synthesis: *A dynamic classroom is not a thing; it is an event.* It is, in the lexicon of many adolescents, a "happening place." It may or may not be a physically attractive place (although, even in the most dilapidated of school buildings, or nearly so, seductive teachers often find ways to make their classrooms physically appealing), but it is always an engaging place. What makes it engaging is that it welcomes students as thinking, feeling, able human beings, and it invites them to use their experiences and languages as tools for learning, not as irrelevances or impertinences to be left in the hallways before entering. It is a place where seductive teachers make it possible for students to become inspired about learning. It is a place where students discover how to feed themselves, to find and to satisfy their hunger as learners.

The school learning environment is a series of events in which everyone—gradually but ultimately—is empowered to succeed. For some, of course, this empowering comes more quickly than for others; but, it is this brand of environment building that must become a top priority for school reform. A "reformed" school is one that teachers and students go to every day, expecting that the events they create and encounter there will *exhilarate* rather than *debilitate* them.

References

Anderson, Maxwell. 1951. *Barefoot in Athens*. New York, NY: William Sloane Associates, Inc.

Clark, David L., and Astuto, Terry A. 1994. "Redirecting Reform: Challenges to Popular Assumptions about Teachers and Students." *Phi Delta Kappan* 75 (7): 513–520.

Decci, Edward L., and Ryan, Richard M. 1990. "A Motivational Approach to Self: Integration in Personality." In *Nebraska Symposium on Motivation 38*, ed. Richard Dienstbier. Lincoln, NB: University of Nebraska Press.

Dickens, Charles. 1958. (originally published in 1854). *Hard Times*. New York, NY: Harper and Row.

Driscoll, Marcy P. 1994. *Psychology of Learning for Instruction*. Boston, MA: Allyn & Bacon.

"49-Member Panel to Draw up Plans for State Education Reform." 1994. *The Virginian-Pilot*, 25 May.

Glass, Jon. 1994. "I'm not Letting the Community off the Hook." *The Virginian-Pilot*, 22 September.

Glasser, William. 1990. *The Quality School*. New York, NY: Harper Perennial.

Kohn, Alfie. 1994. "The Truth about Self-Esteem." *Phi Delta Kappan* 76 (4): 272–283.

Lasley, Thomas. 1987. "Teaching Selflessness in a Selfish Society." *Phi Delta Kappan* 68 (9): 674–678.

Lax, Eric. 1991. *Woody*. New York, NY: Alfred A. Knopf.

Maslow, Abraham. 1943. "A Theory of Human Motivation." *Psychological Review* 50: 370–396.

Nazario, Sonia. 1992. "Right and Wrong: Teaching Values Makes a Comeback." *The Wall Street Journal*, 11 September.

Noddings, Nel. 1992. *The Challenge to Care in Schools: An Alternative Approach to Education*. New York, NY: Teachers College Press.

Postman, Neil. 1979. *Teaching as a Conserving Activity*. New York, NY: Delacorte Press.

Sagan, Carl. 1977. *The Dragons of Eden*. New York, NY: Random House.

Simonds, Robert L. 1994. "A Plea for the Children." *Educational Leadership* 51 (4): 12–15.

Sizer, Theodore. 1984. *Horace's Compromise: The Dilemma of the American High School*. Boston, MA: Houghton Mifflin.

Slade, John. 1994. "Letters from an American Teacher in Russia." Unpublished Manuscript.

Towers, James, M. 1994. "The Perils of Outcome-Based Education." *Phi Delta Kappan* 75 (8): 624–627.

Vines, Vanee. 1994. "Education Task Force Assembles Its Own Recipe for Reform." *The Virginian-Pilot*, 2 September.

"Time to Finance Repairs." 1996. *The Virginian-Pilot*, 24 July.

Wood, George. 1992. *Schools that Work: America's Most Innovative Public Education Programs*. New York, NY: Dutton.

Chapter Six

Becoming a Master Teacher and School Reformer

Over the years, the two of us have taught at several different levels of school. We've taught middle and high school students, as well as undergraduate and graduate students. We've organized and conducted many conferences and workshops for teachers, and we've observed many teachers in kindergarten through university. We've thought, talked, read, and written about the complex art and science of teaching. Our reflections and experiences have led us to a theory of how one grows from novice to expert, from a naturally anxious and tentative beginning teacher to a truly exceptional one.

We believe that this growth involves four phases, or stages.

1. Emulation/Control
2. Experimentation/Discovery
3. Facilitation/Resource
4. Research/Innovation

We aim to couch these phases of growth within the context and principles that inform stage theories of any kind: that is, the stages are hierarchical and teachers pass through them in sequence. One carries each stage with him or her into the next, and it's quite possible to get stuck in a particular stage and never grow beyond it without a lot of help and attention. Moreover, we suggest that the stages are not necessarily bound to years of experience. Some teachers with fewer than, say, five years' experience might operate at the highest levels; other teachers with many more years of experience may get stuck in an early stage. As one of our sharp-tongued colleagues is fond of saying, "Some teachers have had twenty years experience; others have had one year's experience twenty times." We'll describe these stages according to the order in which we think they occur.

First is the stage of Emulation/Control. Regardless of any rebellious streak that may accompany adolescence, it seems that many people tend to choose their long-term work according to the influence of somebody (or several somebodies) whom they have known or admired. For example, how many children of high-profile professional athletes are now professional athletes themselves? What about the children of engineers, doctors, dentists, lawyers, mechanics, shopkeepers, barbers, builders, chefs, soldiers, politicians, clergymen, farmers, and so on? The tendency to follow in the footsteps of significant others is a kind of all-in-the-family phenomenon. It applies to teaching, as well.

It may not be a family member (or admired friend), however, who influences a person to go into teaching; often it's a memorable teacher. Whoever it happens to be, though, the beginning teacher typically uses that person (or persons) as a model. Maybe the model goes all the way back to elementary school, or middle school, or high school, or the university. Regardless of who the model might be, it is that person whom the beginning teacher means to emulate. So in the classroom, for a period of time, the beginning teacher measures himself or herself against that model, consciously or subconsciously.

From the outset, then, the novice teacher has a vision, an image (both sharp and vague), of what he or she is supposed to be and do—how to behave, how to relate to students, even how to move and speak. In this first stage, beginning teachers tend to teach as they were taught. Early into the job, one of the issues that looms largest for the beginning teacher is how to control the class, how to manage things, how to keep everything from getting out of hand or falling apart. Control and classroom management are overriding priorities. The teacher tends to see the classroom as "mine" rather than "ours." In stage one, the novice teacher is so busy trying to follow a model (or models), trying to plan for instruction each day, and trying to keep order in the classroom that he or she seldom gives serious thought to who he or she is as an individual, as a unique human being, as a teacher with a special set of strengths and weaknesses to draw upon and to deal with.

Stage one is a highly self-conscious, survival-oriented stage. The teacher is sensitive to his or her every word and action and to students' *reactions*. The novice teacher does little in the way of profound self-reflection, and if he or she does reflect deeply, it's often of the "woe is me" variety. The main job is to make it through the first day, first week, first semester, first year. It is a pragmatically driven stage; for some it may last less than a year; for others, longer.

Second is the stage of Experimentation/Discovery. The teacher is ready to move out of the Emulation/Control stage when he or she realizes, "I've got to be myself in the classroom, find my own voice, persona, and style." The first stage was useful and instructive, largely because it gave the teacher many rich opportunities to discover what works and doesn't work, at least in "my classroom." Now, however, there is a drive to move on. The teacher is ready for stage two when he or she feels the need to change, to make adjustments. It's time to take some risks, and the teacher feels *nearly* comfortable and *tentatively* excited with the prospect.

Initiating conversations with colleagues about professional subjects and issues, seriously reading some professional literature, attending a few professional conferences, analyzing classroom dynamics on a regular basis—these behaviors signal the teacher's passage into stage two. The teacher may have attempted some of these in stage one largely out of a sense of duty. Now, however, the teacher senses a practical and immediate need to know. He or she begins to engage in professional behaviors beyond the classroom from a sense of informed caring about work.

This is not a stage in which the teacher merely rejects the old models—they are still venerable, honorable, and worthy. While still respecting and honoring them, though, the teacher ventures into unexplored territory and begins to grope for more effective ways to help students learn. The emphasis begins to shift away from "how to make it through the day" to "how to make this is a successful day for *my kids*." Gradually in this stage, the teacher begins to acquire a sense that the classroom belongs to "us" rather than to "me." Everything that has to do with teaching—planning, organizing, reflecting, choosing, adjusting, judging—takes on a new importance and urgency. The stage two teacher is developing an emerging sense of self-confidence.

Everywhere the teacher turns during this stage of growth, everything he or she sees or hears—a restaurant menu, a grocery receipt, a television ad, a song on the radio, vacation slides or film, an antique artifact—becomes a potentially useful tool for teaching something more effectively and seductively. The stage two teacher is a great collector, often a file builder. Coming across novel ideas for fresh teaching methods and learning activities is like getting surprise gifts at Christmas to the teacher in stage two. The appetite for experimentation and discovery seems insatiable.

At the beginning of this stage, the teacher doesn't give much regular, conscious thought to the development of a personal theory of teaching. More deeply into the stage, however, the teacher becomes increasingly aware of the need to articulate what he or she truly believes—about the most effective role of a classroom teacher, about optimal conditions for learning, about how to help every student succeed. Generally, this is a pragmatic period of teacher development, built upon the pragmatism of stage one. It's still a period of "on-the-job training," but the stage two teacher is laying the foundation for making a commitment to teaching as a profession.

Third is the stage of Facilitation/Resource. The teacher takes a step into stage three when he or she feels less egocentrism, or a different kind of egocentrism, about teaching. That is to say, the teacher now feels less need to manage and control every minute and activity that occurs in the classroom. In this stage the teacher is not only willing to allow some spontaneity but is also ready to welcome it, often seeing it as a potential "teachable moment." Of course, the teacher's ego is still involved in what happens, but his or her locus of satisfaction shifts from a feeling that "today *I* performed well" to "today the *students* were engaged." This latter feeling is ego satisfying, too, but in a different way from the former. Also, joint ownership of the classroom is a fully fixed concept and commitment in the mind of a stage three teacher.

Stage three finishes the "letting-go" time. Contrasted with the pragmatism of stages one and two, this stage tends to be philosophy and theory driven. Now the teacher realizes that school should not be a place where young people come to watch old people work. The teacher steps out of the center of things and allows students more freedom to find their own ways as learners. In this stage the teacher begins to develop consciously a theory of teaching, which has been incubating in stage two but now fully emerges; it will continue to evolve, of course, but now it exists as a coherent set of beliefs capable of clear articulation. Whatever the other elements of that theory might be—however it turns out—it will demand a changed role for the teacher: that of a *facilitator* and *resource* person for students. The teacher's role becomes one of guide and helper; and, in the teacher's mind, the student's role becomes one of *active learner*, of worker. There were manifestations of these roles near the end of stage two, but now they appear consistently.

It is at this time that the teacher develops a fuller sense of his or her own strengths and weaknesses. The stage three teacher capitalizes on strengths and works on weaknesses. For example, if the teacher is a strong and charismatic lecturer, he or she may lecture more than another stage three teacher might. Another stage three teacher may have a penchant for sketching and drawing and may use that talent to get across to students what is important for them to learn. (As an analogy, let's say you ask someone for directions to an office building. One person might help you by drawing a perfect and clear map to get you there. Another person might give you oral or written directions that are equally helpful. People have different skills and talents, of course, different ways of communicating and approaching a task.) Stage three teachers have discovered their own special and personal gifts, and they use them to instructional advantage.

We're not saying that stage three teachers find one or two effective ways of teaching and use them exclusively, ad nauseum. On the contrary, a distinguishing trait of the stage three teacher is *flexibility* and a recognition of the curriculum as both a who and a what. The stage three teacher knows that teachers must tell students things, but students must be allowed to tell each other things, too. The stage three teacher recognizes that telling is not nearly enough, that students learn from give-and-take, from conversations, demonstrations, and lots of practice. The stage three teacher recognizes that much evaluative feedback to students (not to be confused with grades) is important to learning. The stage three teacher also recognizes that the classroom is a place for collaboration among all who work there, teachers and students alike.

In sum, the stage three teacher has internalized state-of-the-art and fundamental principles of teaching and learning and has translated them into classroom practice, with both a desire and need to keep searching. Drawing on all of the experimenting, foraging, collecting, and file building that occurred in stage two, the stage three teacher becomes an executive decision maker. He or she picks and chooses what works according to the demands of a given situation and students' needs of the moment.

Fourth is the stage of Research/Innovation. This is the mature "master teacher" stage. The teacher now knows a great deal about how to lead, attract, and win over students to a view of school as a welcoming place, which nurtures their growth. Of course, manifestations of seductive teaching appear often in stage three (flashes may even appear as early as stage one, almost certainly in stage two), but now they appear regularly and consistently rather than occasionally and sporadically. The stage four teacher is centered and in control. (Like a skilled pool player, always thinking several shots ahead to get the best position for the next ball on the table, the master teacher is often anticipating several moves ahead in the classroom.) The stage four teacher realizes that he or she hasn't "arrived," but that the journey will be ongoing, fascinating, and engaging.

In this stage the teacher develops what might be described as a third persona in the classroom. (The first persona is the model or models from stage one, whom the beginning teacher tends to emulate; the second is the teacher's own "true" self that emerges and develops through stages two and three; the third is an attentive spectator—these three begin to become integrated as the teacher moves into and through stage four.) The teacher now is somehow able to stand apart from himself or herself and watch with a critical eye what goes on in the classroom. This third persona watches the second persona teach and assesses the dynamics of the total learning environment—self encounters self; the "I" meets the "I." In this way, the teacher becomes an active researcher within his or her classroom. The emergence of a third persona isn't mystical; it's an emerging ability to act and, at the same time, to assess critically one's actions. (Experts in any field possess the same skill.) When you observe the classroom of a stage four teacher, you know you're in the presence of a confident, exceptional professional, one who truly knows what he or she is about. You're in the presence of *Quality*, and "you know it when you see it."

Stage four is characterized by the teacher's deep reflection and inquiry about how students are trying to learn, how and why some are successful and others are not. The teacher becomes a watchful and skillful researcher in the classroom, which itself becomes a working laboratory in which teachers and students push back the frontiers of knowledge about teaching and learning. Problems are no longer insurmountable obstacles but opportunities and challenges that the teacher and students work out together. As a classroom researcher, the teacher understands how he or she and students will achieve Quality—*by asking questions about how to achieve desired results and by rigorously pursuing the paths to Quality that they invent and discover together.* The stage four teacher has learned that the emphasis in a classroom must always be upon how to achieve desirable ends, upon processes students go through to be successful. The stage four teacher, as classroom researcher, is always examining teaching and learning behaviors, making innovative adjustments and adaptations according to his or her own findings, and probing the classroom culture by working as a learning partner with students.

To teachers in the early stages of growth, emphases are often on ends rather than on means to achieve those ends; that is, on the products of students' learning rather than on the processes that lead to those products. Less mature teachers often use students' products as starting points—for example, marking every error on a piece of student writing, obsessively correcting homework assignments, insisting on a single "right answer" to every question and issue, evaluating tests, assessing lab reports, criticizing individual or group presentations, and the like. Less mature teachers tend to assume that merely pointing out errors is equivalent to teaching, that telling and correcting equal teaching. While alerting students to errors is certainly a necessary task, it seems a disproportionate part of many less mature teachers' fundamental routines.

To state the matter as an aphorism, the stage four teacher knows that "an ounce of prevention is worth a pound of cure," that the greatest amount of time and energy in a classroom must go to providing help and instruction to students *as* they work rather than *after* they work. When students have created their products or taken tests, teachers must evaluate, of course; but, the most fruitful labor, as the stage four teacher knows, lies in creating conditions in classrooms that enable everyone to assist everyone else on the way toward those products and tests. In such a classroom, the product or the test, when each arrives, is always more satisfying, a kind of celebration of learning.

The debate over what or who should be at the center of a learning environment continues among educators and policymakers. It seems interminable. Some school observers believe the teacher should occupy the center of the classroom; some, the paper curriculum; some, the test; some, the student; and others, the mores, values, and expectations of the community that the school serves. The stage four teacher no longer worries about what or who is at the center. The stage four teacher knows that *everything and everyone is and should be at the center of a classroom learning environment at the same time.* Stage four teachers have achieved a sense of integration in their educational philosophies and classroom practices, and they plan and behave accordingly. They know that they themselves, the curriculum, the students, the tests, and the community are all present in the classroom every day *at its center.* All are acknowledged, honored, and accommodated, and seductive teachers attempt to meet that complex challenge, a challenge borne of the realization that any classroom learning environment is a social/political/economic series of events that often influence learning outcomes.

In summary, teachers at the highest level of development have become sophisticated students of teaching. They have integrated teaching and learning into a single concept, and their classrooms testify to that integration. Everyone in those rooms is a teacher, and everyone is a learner. Stage four teachers know that the results of student learning always will be more positive when students receive the right help at the right time, when they actively work together to create their learning products, and when they demonstrate their learning through various kinds of assessment procedures.

Stage four teachers have a clear conception of Quality, and in their presence, you both see and feel it. Stage four teachers are master teachers, researchers within the complex classroom environments where they and their students work each day. They are ready and able to step outside those classrooms to lead, attract, and win over other teachers in their quest toward becoming seductive teachers, as well. Here are three examples of such teachers at work.

Ed Jacob is a veteran drama and speech teacher. As a drama coach, director, speech teacher, and actor himself, he is aware of the importance of involving students actively in the processes of their learning. Jacob takes students where they would not go without his help. As he puts it, "I see the classroom as a 'mind-field,' and my job is to set off small explosions."

As we sit in his Drama 1 class on a fall day, we look around at the physical learning environment. A small built-in stage area takes up one side of the room, with the teacher's desk located in a corner near the door. The desk is cluttered with books and folders of students' work. There are no typical students' desks; instead, there are plywood tables and plastic-back chairs. It has taken Jacob more than a year to get this room "just the way my students and I need it to be," but he has persisted and it shows. Bulletin boards occupy nearly all available wall space, decorated with programs of Broadway plays, programs and posters of past class performances for school and community groups, and various masks. There are no windows. The fluorescent lights flicker.

As students gather, Ed Jacob closes the door, moves to the chalkboard, and writes one word in large letters, "Tableau." He says the word aloud and walks slowly around the room, selecting one student from each of four groups arranged in clusters at their plywood tables. He ushers the chosen students to the stage, as others shift in their chairs to get a good look at the group of four. He points to a pile of objects on the wooden platform—assorted lengths of gray styrofoam pipe insulation, some nylon ropes, pieces of PVC pipes, two plastic buckets, and some colorful fabric remnants.

Jacob says to the group, "Your job is to find a way to use these materials to create a series of still-life scenes that will tell a story." He turns to the rest of the class and says, "In your groups—including those of you on the stage—come up with a few stories that are familiar to all of you." After allowing time for some small-group discussion, he asks, "What do you have?" Shortly, Jacob and the class as a whole negotiate an agreement upon four scenarios among the many they suggested: the D-Day invasion, the discovery of fire, humans landing on the moon, and Little Red Riding Hood. Jacob asks each group to choose one of the stories and discuss how they might tell it through a sequence of four still-life scenes. As the other groups imagine their scenarios, the group on the stage works with their artifacts.

After about twenty minutes, the stage group is ready to act out its story. Jacob says to the rest of the class, "Play the good audience, and as you watch the performance take note of how these actors have chosen to tell their tale. What do they include and exclude? We'll talk about it when they're done." As the group begins to work, it becomes obvious that they have chosen the discovery of fire scenario, which they reveal in four silent still-life scenes. The class discusses what they have witnessed, raising questions, and asking for clarification of some of the scenes. Jacob then says, "Tomorrow we'll see this story played out again, after some time at the beginning of class to make any adjustments the group wishes to make. We'll see each of your other group's stories played out, as well. Bring any props you think you'll need for your performances. We'll discuss each group's original effort, and all will have a chance to show your work twice. Also for tomorrow—come prepared to talk about the meaning of *tableau*."

"I see the classroom as a 'mind-field,' and my job is to set off small explosions." We have seen Ed Jacob's basic philosophy of teaching stated in his own metaphoric way, played out literally in this Drama 1 class. He is a teacher who has gone beyond the teller stage of teaching to reach the student-invention-and-discovery stage, and he is able to lead, win over, and attract students to this way of learning.

In *Horace's Compromise*, Theodore Sizer speaks of the teacher's craft this way, "Teaching, of course, is a form of theater. While the point is to have the students learn, the teacher has to explain, provoke, cajole, inspire, criticize, demand, love" (1984, 153). Ed Jacob's students experience these behaviors and qualities during their time with him each day. They take risks in his class because they know that's what he expects; they prepare for class and become engaged, as well. They work hard to do their best because they know they will have more than one chance to "make it right." The role that Ed Jacob consistently plays in his classroom, a role made believable by the energy and quality of his students' work, is that of the seductive teacher.

Charles Jarvis, an English and social studies teacher for more than twenty years, is a master of classroom organization. He thinks of himself as "more of a traditional teacher." Jarvis developed a practical way to involve students directly in the process of determining their own grades. At the beginning of each nine-week term, he asks students to enter into a contract with him and their parents (or guardians) for the grades they want. While the idea of contract grading isn't new, Jarvis found how to make it work more satisfactorily for both him and his students. One learning contract he uses involves the following general activities: reading, writing, collaborative projects, and testing. While he varies the specific conditions of the contract from class to class and from one grading term to another, a prototype from one of his eleventh-grade, mixed-ability English classes illustrates how his system works.

In a unit on Civil War literature, Jarvis asks students to read beyond the standard textbook. For an A, students might read five articles and one book by or about a Civil War writer or figure; for a B, they might read five articles; for a C, they might read three. (Students are individually responsible for finding articles and books in the school media center; Jarvis provides a beginning list.) They are held accountable for their readings by submitting to him written reports (critiques), in which they indicate what they liked and didn't like, as well as some new insight or further understanding that they lacked previously. (Written reports that Jarvis finds unacceptable are returned to students for revision; reports must be judged acceptable by the end of the term period, according to specific criteria.)

To meet the writing condition, students must do the following: for an A, they submit three acceptable essays on different topics or issues; for a B, they submit two; for a C, they submit one. During the grading term, he gives students class time to read and respond to each other's essays to increase the likelihood that what he finally receives from each student is at least a second draft effort. As he is the final arbiter of acceptability, he returns to students any unacceptable pieces for them to continue to work on until the last week of the grading term. The number of acceptable pieces he has from each student at the end determines the degree to which a student meets the conditions of this contract element. (For example, a student who contracted for an A may have written only two, not three, acceptable essays by the end of the grading term, in which case the student's overall grade may be lowered.)

For the collaborative requirement, Jarvis allows students to organize their own groups (usually two to five students per cluster), with each choosing a different topic to present to the class. Each group submits its topic to him for approval, and he reserves the right to negotiate. Jarvis establishes a calendar on which he schedules each group's presentation to the class, spread out over the course of the grading term. During actual presentations, each group member must participate actively, show evidence of research, and communicate to the class in a reasonably clear and knowledgeable manner. For an A per group member, the presentation will last about thirty minutes; for a B, about twenty; for a C, about ten.

Students take two major tests during the grading period, one at the midpoint and one at the end. Material for which students are responsible comes from their assigned textbook reading, as well as Jarvis's lectures and class discussions. The tests tend to include multiple choice and short essay items. For an A, students must have an average grade on the two tests of at least ninety; for a B, an average of at least eighty; and for a C, at least seventy.

Here are examples of what students might show at the end of the grading term to earn their grades. A-contract students must show evidence of having read five articles and one book, written three acceptable essays on different topics, participated in a thirty-minute group presentation to the class, and made at least a ninety average on two tests. B-contract students show evidence of having read five articles, written two acceptable essays, participated in a twenty-minute group presentation to the class, and made at least an eighty average on two tests. C-contact students show evidence of having read three articles, written one acceptable essay, participated in a ten-minute group presentation to the class, and made at least a seventy average on two tests. (Students are able to contract for an A, B, or C—no lower. To get a D or an F, a student must not meet the conditions of a C contract.)

The basic mechanics of creating the contracts goes something like this. At the beginning of a grading term, students decide on grades for which they wish to contract. They then sign their contracts, the teacher signs them, and parents or guardians sign them. (After each component on the contract form, there is a space for students and parents or guardians to sign, to keep everyone involved during the course of fulfilling all contract work.) If a student does not live up to one or more conditions of the signed contract, the contract is broken and Jarvis determines the grade. Teacher judgment remains critical in this approach, as it does in any other process or system of assigning grades. Sometimes a student who contracted for an A may get an A-minus or a B—sometimes lower. On occasion, a student may exceed his or her contract, in which case a student who, let's say, contracted for a C may get a C-plus or a B. Charles Jarvis declares, "Teaching must inspire individual initiative and responsibility, not to mention good decision making and problem solving. Everything I've done in my classroom has been geared to helping students develop these qualities and skills. I encourage students always to go for high-grade contracts, but ultimately it's up to them. By the second semester, nearly everyone is going for As and Bs." At the center of this teacher's classroom is everything at once: the paper curriculum, the student, the parent, the teacher, and the test. All are integrated, and Charles Jarvis's efforts, regarded by some as "conservative," are exemplary in this regard.

Ken Salbu, an English teacher, is a person with an intense need for order. As he puts it, "It's a matter of my own brain chemistry. I don't like clutter, chaos, and confusion." He goes on, "My growth as a teacher has been an odyssey toward satisfying *my* need for order and my *students'* need for freedom." In his early stages of development, his main goal was to "cover the curriculum" in the conventional sense. An observation from Henry David Thoreau's *Walden* helped him take a more expanded view of his mission as a teacher, "We do not ride upon the railroad; it rides upon us," said Thoreau (1962, 90). Salbu began to look for ways to ride upon the curriculum rather than let the curriculum ride upon him and his students. As a result, his perspective shifted.

Now Ken Salbu's classroom often has a workshop atmosphere. It is a place that encourages independence. It is a laboratory which, in Salbu's words, has created "a liberation from constraint which allows students to flourish." He recognizes the curriculum as both a what and a who—content and concepts of English to be learned and students who must do the learning. He has grown beyond the early stages of teaching, in which he says he spent much time "prescribing and describing, assignment after assignment," to reach higher stages in which he now makes far more interrogative statements in class than declarative and imperative ones. His classroom is filled with books from *The U.S. Coast Guard Survival Manual* to Charles Dickens' *Great Expectations* and Bram Stoker's *Dracula*. His classroom library grows and changes every year. Standard literature anthologies and grammar/composition textbooks line up on wall shelves for students to use as needs arise. Salbu is a leader, resource person, researcher, and innovator in his classroom, and his students are active learners who must make decisions and solve problems for themselves.

One day of observation in Salbu's classroom gives testimony to his status as a master teacher. A forty-one minute class period begins with a mini lesson of about ten minutes, followed by a student workshop. The mini lesson begins with Salbu telling his students about a writing assignment he gave to another class many years ago. He switches on an overhead projector to show the assignment. It's a paragraph that offers some critical commentary on Jack London's novel *The Call of the Wild*, which his current students have been reading. The last sentence of the assignment reads this way, "In a separate paragraph for each, characterize five of the most important dogs in the novel." The class is amused.

Salbu says, "I really gave a group of seventh graders this writing assignment. What do you think of it?" One student says, "Mr. Salbu, did anybody write a good paper off that?" Another adds, "What did you mean by 'characterize'?" Salbu switches off the overhead projector. He nods to his students, silently inviting more comments and questions. Students express some relief that they do not have to write an essay on this topic, one that may have little connection to their own thoughtful responses to London's novel. Salbu now shifts the focus to a discussion of *The Call of the Wild*, which students have read as a class.

"Well, what do *you* make of this novel?" he asks. Students talk about the qualities of leadership that the dog Buck possesses in the book; about how Buck's capture is like the slavery of African Americans in colonial times; about the need for laws to protect the weak against unjust treatment by a powerful few; about whether it is always wrong to steal (as Buck stole food to survive); about what team work means; about the gentle relationship between the dog Buck and a man named Thornton, who gave him his freedom; about the need for *mutual respect*. The role Salbu chooses for himself in this open discussion is to recognize students who wish to talk, ask questions, insert his own views occasionally, and encourage students to express their ideas more fully.

As we watch and listen to this classroom discussion, we are reminded of something John Steinbeck wrote. In "About Ed Ricketts," from *Sea of Cortez*, Steinbeck said this about his marine biologist friend,

> Everyone near him was influenced by him, deeply and permanently. Some he taught how to think, others how to see or hear. Children on the beach he taught how to look for and find beautiful animals in worlds they had not suspected were there at all. *He taught everyone without seeming to*." (1951, x, xi)

What Ken Salbu was doing in this mini lesson was precisely that—*teaching without seeming to.* He was inviting students to make personal responses to their reading, and from those responses he pushed students to think critically and creatively. Finally, their responses to the book will be shaped by each other's views, and their writing will become a synthesis of their comprehensive ideas. Students are building their own interpretive community here.

As his students prepare for the workshop segment of this class, Salbu says they can use their time to discuss, plan, or begin to draft their responses to Jack London's novel. Students who are actually writing may meet with him if necessary. Students seem to know they need to think, reread, talk among themselves, and write during the workshop. Salbu sets a deadline of three days for students to produce a complete first draft of their responses to the book. There is no objecting or complaining among students about the work they've been asked to do. It is clear they are used to what routinely goes on and what is expected. They have been operating this way for months now.

While students work, Salbu sits at a small round table in the corner of the room near his desk. On this table is an assortment of paper, markers, pens, glue, magazines, staplers, scissors, tape, folders, hole punchers, and other supplies arranged neatly for students' use. Some take a few supplies, some talk in pairs or larger groups, some begin to write. Some wish to confer with Salbu about what they're writing. The teacher listens more than talks as he meets with several students who approach his table in turn. He responds to questions with other questions, unless students clearly need answers and specific direction. The bell rings and the workshop is over for today. There will be other workshops, an average of about three per week.

In Ken Salbu's classes, students behave as real readers and writers, not merely students of reading and writing. They are indeed covering the paper curriculum, but they are doing so in ways that are engaging and in ways that acknowledge and include their own personal agenda as thinking, feeling human beings. Ken Salbu has resolved his old tension between his "need for order" and his students' "need for freedom." The result of this fusion is ego satisfying and healthy for everyone involved. Through interactions with students marked by gentle probing, pointed questions, and thoughtful suggestions, Ken Salbu runs a Quality classroom, and he creates a jointly owned community of learners. It is a community characterized by mutual respect and a sense that everyone is a potential contributor to everyone else's learning.

These three teachers whose work we've described are strong but quite different personalities, with their own uniquely effective teaching styles. They have a combined history of over seventy-five years of teaching experience among them. They have distinguished themselves in the schools where they have taught. We have watched them work on many occasions; we have interviewed them; we have spent many days and evenings discussing their teaching with them; we have corresponded with them; and we have followed their careers for years. We understand and respect the deep commitments they have given to their students, and we celebrate their accomplishments.

These three, truly, are representative cases only. Like them, many other outstanding teachers labor with spark and intensity each day in classrooms throughout the United States, working in different but equally effective ways, to the substantial benefit of students and communities. Regardless of the conditions under which they work, however hospitable and supportive or however difficult, seductive teachers find the wherewithal to do their jobs well. A singular message of this book is, as a profession and as a society, we must find ways to charge such teachers with assisting their colleagues in growing to the stages of teacher development that these teachers have reached. Nothing short of massive increases in the number of seductive teachers in schools will make school reform successful. The best teachers of teachers are master teachers. They must be allowed to share what they know, even *charged* with doing so.

While much of the current news about education is admittedly depressing, stories of seductive teachers appear frequently in the media—stories about teachers of different disciplines and at all levels of school. If you watch, read, and listen carefully, you might change your mind some (if it needs changing) about how the media report only "bad news." Perhaps surprisingly, uplifting and encouraging reports of seductive teaching occur regularly. Before we leave our catalogue of seductive teachers and their special achievements, we'll sample just three more instances from popular press reports.

Michael Ryan, in *Parade Magazine*, writes about the work of Kay Toliver, a teacher of mathematics at P.S. 72/East Harlem Tech in one of New York City's most rundown neighborhoods. Toliver says, "If students make an error in class, I try to spare them the embarrassment that students generally feel. I try to make sure they don't think they can never get the answer. *We work from their mistakes...* Coming from this community, kids don't necessarily hear wonderful things about what they can do" (1994, 14). Yet, Toliver's students go on to a variety of prestigious colleges and universities. In June, 1994, one of her students invited her to graduation at Brown University. In 1992, Toliver was selected the nation's Outstanding Teacher of Mathematics through the Walt Disney Company's American Teacher Awards competition.

While awards and recognition are satisfying to any professional, one of the most significant events in Kay Toliver's teaching life has to do with her role in her school's efforts to improve itself. For a year, she was asked to work strictly with other teachers in her school, helping them to grow to the stage of teacher development that she herself had reached. She was released from her own teaching duties to do so. She says of that experience, "I loved it. I was in classrooms every day. *I wanted to convince teachers that they should be risk-takers.* I wanted to bring some of the joy I feel to them" (14). As of this writing, she is back in her own eighth-grade classroom, helping students invent and discover their own conceptual understandings of mathematics.

The example of Kay Toliver can be played out in all schools. There are teachers in schools everywhere who can be the linchpins of school reform, if given the recognition, the opportunity, and the charge to do so. These are teachers who may never receive national awards; nevertheless, they are seductive teachers who have learned how to raise teaching to the level of sophisticated art and science. They must be enabled to help other teachers do the same.

For another example, we go from Harlem in New York City to Grayson County in a rural mountain area of southwest Virginia, where Gary Horton teaches economics at Grayson County High School. Some years back, according to an article entitled "Real-World Economics" in the *Virginia Journal of Education*, Horton was asked to develop a year-long elective course in economics, with one catch—for financial reasons, there would be no textbooks. So Horton set about creating projects for students that would involve them directly as economists, not just students of economics.

One project students undertook was inspired by a real estate agent's visit as a guest speaker in Horton's class. When the agent told him that there was no existing flyer or brochure that told prospective property buyers about Grayson County, Horton and his students offered to create something to fill the space. The students set about putting together facts and figures, drawn largely from primary sources within the community. They asked themselves questions about the county, its people, events, jobs, and culture, and they conducted research to find answers. They solicited local businesses to pay for production costs, and in 1994 they were able to print 3,000 brochures at a cost of $1,700, with the class raising all but $200 of that amount, which the printing company agreed to contribute. Horton says, "Now the kids have a better understanding of our county and its assets, and they're helping to get people to come and see us. Tourism is one of our biggest businesses. . . . I try to stress to students that they're part of the community, and that they have a responsibility to . . . that community" (1994, 17). This illustration is one of many such projects that make up Horton's economics curriculum, which continues to evolve.

Gary Horton is a risk-taking, innovative teacher who behaves as a researcher within his own classroom. He models the qualities he wishes his students to acquire, and he helps them grow as independent individuals and as contributing citizens to their community. He involves students in the processes of their own learning—active thinking rather than passive absorbing. Teachers like Horton are doing work in their classrooms that must be shared—not so much the products of that work but the processes for getting it done. School reform efforts can transform schooling, but only if they involve seductive teachers in creating the transformation.

Our last example is a bit different from the rest. While the teachers we have described thus far work either in middle schools or high schools, Theofilo Ruiz is a college teacher in Brooklyn. He is a recipient of an award for outstanding teaching, given by the Carnegie Foundation for the Advancement of Teaching, carrying a $5,000 prize. His field is history, and on the night he was to be recognized for his teaching award by the trustees of City University of New York, he could not attend. It was Halloween, and he had a class to teach—a class on witches and wizards. Thirty-five students were enrolled, and he could not disappoint them.

Writing about Ruiz in *The New York Times*, Michael T. Kaufman gives an account of this Halloween class. Before the class began, Ruiz was playing taped operatic arias for his students. The teacher walked among them, giving out trick-or-treat Munchkins, and he launched into a lecture about the origin, history, and significance of Halloween. As Kaufman writes, ". . . he lectured without notes, walking through the rows of students like a preacher or nightclub comic, but offering facts, ideas and insights about the Middle Ages with the same enthusiasm with which he had given out doughnuts." Kaufman's impression was that Ruiz "took his students and his subject more seriously than he took himself" (1994, 27). Although he has taught at Brooklyn for over twenty years, Ruiz claims that he is still "thrilled" by his students.

In accepting his Carnegie award, Ruiz quoted from Bernard of Clarivaux, a twelfth-century Cistercian reformer," . . . there are . . . some who seek knowledge in order to edify others. That is love." It is this brand of love that goes a long way toward defining seductive teaching. For teachers like Ruiz and others we have cited, to lead, win over, and attract students to seeing school (at any level) as a safe place, which welcomes them and nurtures their growth means loving the act of teaching and everything it involves. It means loving how they teach and whom they teach. Such love as this can be contagious.

When seductive teachers work with other teachers, the contagion spreads. As this phenomenon occurs, teachers can grow to higher stages of development. As seductive teachers tell other teachers about what they teach, how they teach, and whom they teach—with a love that undergirds the telling and the showing— these other teachers become not only inspired but challenged to do better. Students benefit, and the nation benefits.

School reform efforts can harness and use these precious and natural resources. Teachers like the ones we have identified—and there are many more throughout the land—can lead school reform that truly affects what happens in classrooms. That, finally, is what school reform must be about—not just politics and warmed-over remedies for problems that demand ingenuity, but serious attention to the work of professional teachers who have found some significant answers to questions and practices that assist student learning. No one has more credibility with teachers than master teachers have.

Seductive teachers, equipped with the results of their own classroom-based research, can present evidence that what they do with students works. When other teachers see that evidence, they may or they may not be immediately instructed by it; over time, though, many will grow. They will grow because of their gradual and regular interaction with seductive teachers. The same qualities that enable such teachers to lead, win over, and attract students also enable them to lead, win over, and attract colleagues.

Lasting, substantial, and effective school reform can never result from fiats and mandates by those who do not work with students in classrooms every day. It will result from the persuasive powers of master teachers, helping their colleagues to invent and discover ways of improving student learning. The most effective school reform efforts, then, will have teachers at the center, teachers who know how to communicate with their colleagues and how to help them grow.

In summary, then, we'll pose two questions and offer some suggested answers.

1. As teachers, what might all of us do in our schools to bring about significant improvement?

2. How might we lead, attract, and win over our colleagues to doing better work?

Here are some possibilities and proposals.

- *Don't coerce.* No professional wants to feel externally pressured to do much of anything. While many people claim, "I work better under pressure," probably few of us actually do. If we listen to our colleagues and then feel we have other (better) answers or solutions to problems and issues, we can offer our thoughts as rationally and articulately as we are able, but we can't do much more. If we invite colleagues into our worlds, we can never be sure they will come, but it's unlikely that we can drag them kicking and screaming. Even if we could, nothing productive would happen when we got them there. Attempting to make people do something—even if we know "it's good for them"—almost never works over the long haul. This principle applies to students and colleagues alike. But perseverance and patience are essential; when we issue invitations, they should be standing invitations.

- *When asked, help.* Not everyone does, you know. We've all had colleagues who seem to work hard at remaining isolated in their classrooms and their schools, for a variety of reasons—some people just feel uncomfortable about sharing with others what they think and do. Such people often avoid placing themselves in situations where they may be asked for help, and they are not inclined to ask others for help. But we cannot lead if we do not help, if we do not share with others what we know and do. Leaders and helpers in schools are known by such comments as, "(so-and-so) can always be counted on, turned to, depended on, approached, trusted," or ". . . is always *there.*" Teachers as school reformers will be counted in this latter group.

- *Relate to colleagues as you relate to students.* We don't mean that we should treat our colleagues like children. What we *do* mean is that we should offer our colleagues the same respect, encouragement, help, freedom, concern, modeling, and professional behavior that we offer our students each day in the classroom. Enough said.

- *Suggest agenda items for faculty gatherings.* We've all complained about faculty meetings and other such gatherings that focus solely on "administrivia." Sometimes, though, the fault may be ours. A worthwhile project might be to figure out how to approach whom about getting more teacher input into the making of agenda items for any and all faculty gatherings. What we are after, of course, is time to discuss items (issues, ideas, problems, questions) that pertain *directly* to helping teachers and students do better work.

- *Resist reform strategies you don't believe in.* This is a tricky one, of course. It has to do with "don't coerce." Sometimes we feel coerced by forces beyond us, sometimes nameless and faceless forces, to conform to reform strategies we had no voice in making and no confidence in implementing. It may be a bit bravado to take the position that "we don't get paid enough to do what we don't believe in," because most of us actually need to work! Yet, if we honestly and rationally recoil from some "reform" idea in our school, if we truly believe it will not help us and our students do better work, we should make our objections heard as effectively as we know how. If we are known to be good at what we do, if we are known to be "team players," if we are a presence in our schools, if we don't cry "wolf" too often, we can sometimes win our points. Not always, but sometimes. But we can't ever win at all if we don't participate in the conversation—the conversation that counts and that is potentially productive, not just the conversation in whispers and shouts that often occur in remote corners of the teachers' lounge.

- *Conduct classroom-based research and share it.* Speaking of the teachers' lounge, it may be a good place to share what we're finding from rigorous "kid watching" in our classrooms. As we closely observe learners, register our observations, ask questions we truly need to answer, revise instructional approaches, and now and then make breakthroughs to students, we create the grist for making things better in our schools. What better way to lead our colleagues than to share the hard-won results of research labors in our classrooms and to model this high-level professional behavior through dialogue and conversation with one or more fellow faculty?

- *Join a National Writing Project site.* We've devoted an entire chapter to extolling the virtues of the National Writing Project, so we need little more elaboration here. The NWP is a teachers-teaching-teachers model of faculty development, and its summer institutes and year-long networking activities give teachers a keener sense of professionalism. If there are other such projects you know of, join them, too. Active membership in professional organizations of teachers is essential, as well.

- *Don't say "no" to leadership opportunities.* We have a colleague who volunteers for everything. Once, during a period of good-natured ribbing about this habit, she responded, "I'd rather *do* it than have it done *to* me!" If leadership opportunities come along that might result in making a school's learning environment better, we should seize them. Chairing curriculum committees, faculty development committees, self-study committees, and special project committees can be important, productive work. Agreeing to speaking engagements and conducting workshops in schools, school districts, and communities can bring big payoffs in terms of greater support for teachers and students in general. Good leadership is often a silent, invisible, behind-the-scenes enterprise, but it sometimes needs to "go public," as well.

- *Promote cross-visitations in teachers' classrooms.* This is an old idea, but a good one. Inviting a teacher to your classroom to give you a response to something you're doing with students is a desirable start, and it may lead to a reciprocal invitation. Actually watching our colleagues teach and having them watch us teach can break down walls that inhibit healthy, collegial relationships and conversations among faculty in a school. Showing is nearly always better than telling, and collaborative, professional endeavors can lead to everyone doing better work individually.

- *Get to know influential people who can help.* There's a true story of a college professor who had a new dean in his college of education. When one of his colleagues asked, "Have you met the new dean?" he replied, "No. I figure this dean will last about five years, so let me tell you my ambition. Five years from now, after she's moved on, she'll be at a conference somewhere, and someone will ask if she knew me when she was here. And she'll say, 'Did I know *who*?'" Well, that's an appropriate ambition if you wish to be a fly on the wall, but it doesn't help otherwise. In part, to be influential, one must know as well as possible influential people—the principal, the superintendent, central office staff, the school board, community business persons and leaders, state department of education staff, and politicians. Such people can be supportive professionally and even financially, and that's not bad. If your relationship with an influential person can help your school, colleagues, and kids, that relationship is worth cultivating. And who knows? You might even find you *like* influential people—some of them, anyway.

- *Communicate regularly with parents.* We know outstanding teachers who send letters to parents at the beginning of every school year. The letter gives information about the teachers' personal and professional backgrounds (e.g., married with kids of their own, perhaps; the highest education degree they have; how long in teaching; maybe references to some outstanding achievements; etc.), and then briefly explains educational philosophy, expectations of students, and how the teaching will go in the year ahead (e.g., how to teach reading and writing, etc.). Teachers who send such letters often declare that the practice helps build personal credibility and significant partnerships with parents. Also, it sometimes heads off potential problems or complaints that spring from a lack of communication, information, and prejudice. Such letters seem desirable and worth the time and trouble, but so do phone calls, e-mails, and other types of opportunities for communication with parents. The idea, of course, is to establish partnerships, and sometimes that's a challenge. But it's impossible without trying.

- *Promote/organize teacher-led seminars.* Again, without being too pushy about it, working to create opportunities to *raise the level of professional conversation* in a school is a noble and desirable enterprise. Inviting teachers to your room for after-school meetings on occasion, or even to a favorite watering hole or cafe off school grounds, can result in reciprocal invitations and regular opportunities to learn from one another. We know many teachers who do this, and often "rules" get established, such as, "For the first fifteen minutes we agree to vent job-related frustrations; for the next fifteen we discuss a professional topic of interest; and the last fifteen, it's all personal; then we go home, feeling better." More formal seminars can also be useful and instructive. Organizing a teacher group to meet once a month, perhaps, taking turns at leading the discussion of a topic or sharing a classroom idea/experience, can be a significant contribution to teacher growth and school-wide improvement.

- *Invite nonteaching staff to participate in classrooms.* From the principal and guidance counselors to the custodial and cafeteria staff, asking individuals who work in schools to participate in the instructional and learning lives of teachers and students builds team spirit and a healthy school climate. Problems created by differentiated jobs in a school can often be overcome when everyone has a central focus—the education of children in a place where everyone plays a special role but also has knowledge about and interest in one another's roles. Some visitors to the classroom might simply wish to observe; others might want to participate more actively. Either way is acceptable.

- *Build a reputation as the best listener in your school.* How many good listeners do you know? Are you a good listener yourself? While talking with Mr. Spencer in Salinger's *The Catcher in the Rye*, Holden Caulfield observes this about his old teacher at Pencey Prep, "He wasn't even listening. He hardly ever listened to you when you said something" (1945, 10). The society as a whole seems neither to expect or promote good listening. Have you noticed that nearly any time you hear an announcement over a public address system, it gets repeated? What if newspapers printed every sentence twice in succession? The so-called crisis in reading and writing may be nothing compared to the crisis in listening. So we should all make ourselves better listeners. To do so requires concentration, that's all. Still, concentration takes discipline and the determination to let our own thoughts drop to the cranial floor when someone else is talking. But the payoffs for good listening are enormous, in the classroom and throughout the school. Good leadership often begins with good listening. Newt Gingrich is right about that.

- *Work visibly.* This last suggestion nearly amounts to a synthesis of the previous fourteen. It is conventional wisdom in the "leadership industry," and it is sound wisdom, indeed. It has often escaped teachers, even the best ones. Inner demons that keep some of us from acting on it say things to us like, "Don't call attention to yourself," or "Don't brag," or "Don't toot your own horn." Yet, leadership requires some degree of assertiveness, and assertiveness often requires being seen and heard. Modeling is a powerful teaching device, with both students and colleagues, and self-promotion is a desirable activity if it also results in student promotion, colleague promotion, and school promotion. If it's done in a spirit of making conditions better for everybody, self-promotion never requires an apology.

References

Kaufman, Michael. 1994. "Lighting Up Dark Ages, and Education Itself." *The New York Times*, 5 November.

"Real-World Economics." 1994. *Virginia Journal of Education* 88 (3): 16–20.

Ryan, Michael. 1994. "Her Kids Love Math." *Parade Magazine*, 16 October.

Salinger, J.D. 1945. *The Catcher in the Rye*. New York, NY: Bantam Books.

Sizer, Theodore. 1984. *Horace's Compromise: The Dilemma of the American High School*. Boston, MA: Houghton Mifflin.

Steinbeck, John, and Ricketts, Ed. 1951. *Sea of Cortez*. New York, NY: Viking Press.

Thoreau, Henry David. 1962. *Walden*. New York, NY: Time Inc. (Originally published in 1854.)